COUSIN AMELIA

COUSIN AMELIA

Stories of Amelia Earhart's Adventurous Family

ERNST F. TONSING

LUMINARE PRESS

WWW.LUMINAREPRESS.COM

To all who turn their eyes to the skies
and envy the birds.

TABLE OF CONTENTS

INTRODUCTION

For many, the life of Amelia Earhart is a mystery. How could a young girl, born in a town in Kansas, grow up to become one of the most accomplished and admired women in the world? What led her to attain such achievements? In her day, women were mostly homebound and restricted to family activities. Who then served as her role models? What contributed to that marvelous mix of spirit and energy that was Amelia Earhart?

I am a second cousin of Amelia, but one generation down. I never met Amelia, nor her father, Ed Earhart, but I did know her mother, Amy, whom we used to visit when she was living in Southern California. Amy's mother was the cousin of my grandmother, Ruth Martin Tonsing. Grandmother Tonsing was not only a cousin of Amy, but they also were good friends. I spent much time with grandmother, talking about all sorts of subjects, but especially the family. I remember stories she used to tell about Amelia, some of them so funny that it is hard not to laugh out loud when I think about them.

There were two important factors that may answer these questions. The first was the discipline she was taught as a child in her grandparents' house in Atchison, Kansas. Amelia Earhart grew up in the late Victorian Age when children were brought up with certain expectations and training. In this way she learned a system of values, developed self-control, self-motivation, how to remain cool at all times, and gained emotional stability.

Role models within Amelia Earhart's family also played a part. I have over forty books about Amelia in my library. They describe her career, her planes, and, most of all, the mystery of her disappearance, but few mention except briefly the remarkable individuals that populated her family. The direct and indirect influence of family was central and enduring in Amelia's life. They provided her with role models during her formative years. Amelia absorbed the accounts of her ancestors, her mother's and father's parents, her prominent Aunt Harriet, and her other relatives. She internalized their values and sense of justice and compassion in a way that not only sustained her as an adult, but also provided the foundation for her achievements.

I interviewed Amelia's blood relatives for their recollections about their famous kin. I talked with cousins Beatrice "Beatsie" Challiss Laws, Beatsie's sister Catherine "Tiffy" Challiss Cappel, and Paul Martin Tonsing Jr. who knew Amelia. I also talked with Robert Tonsing Jr., Dorothy Linn, Rebecca Chaky, Richard Tonsing, and other family members to learn the stories about Amelia that they remembered.

When I was about twelve years old, Grandmother Tonsing handed me a long letter she had received from Amy Earhart to copy. It related many extraordinary stories about her ancestors. Later, Louise Foudray, former director of the Amelia Earhart Birthplace Museum in Atchison, Kansas, was kind enough to send me a photocopy of the journal of Amelia's grandfather, David Earhart, that contained many more accounts of the family. From the letter, journal, and stories, the following chapters have been written that they might contribute to the body of knowledge about America's beloved aviatrix and illuminate the heart of the Amelia Earhart we know and love.

Ernst F. Tonsing

Chapter One

THE MAKING OF A HERO

Home of Amelia and Alfred Otis,
ca. 1910, birthplace of Amelia Earhart
Photograph by Ruth Martin Tonsing

T rue heroes are always in short supply. They are people who are noted for their courage, their abilities, and their excellence of character. People are drawn to them, admire them, and wish to be like them.

So many heroes are found to have "feet of clay," however, of having some fundamental flaw, revealing that they are not worthy of people's esteem. There is one hero, however, who has measured up, and whose reputation has increased not only in America but around the world, and she is Amelia Earhart.

After Wilbur and Orville Wright flew the first machine-powered plane on December 17, 1903, there were a number of women who took to the air: Emma Lilian Todd both designed and flew her own airplanes beginning in 1908. Todd also made the first parachute jump from a plane in 1908, and by the time she retired in 1922, she had completed 1,100 jumps.

Still others were French citizen Raymonde de Laroche, the world's first licensed woman pilot in 1910; Blanche "Betty" Stuart Scott, the American daredevil pilot; Bessica Raiche the first woman to make a solo flight; Harriet Quimby the first licensed female pilot in the United States in 1911, and the first woman to cross the English Channel by plane in 1912; Canadian-American Matilde E. Moisant, who broke a world altitude record in 1911; the air stunt-woman, Phoebe Jane Fairgrave Omlie, licensed in 1920; Ethel "Ethel Dare" Gilmore Johnson, the first woman who walked from the wing of one plane to another in 1920; Bessie Coleman, known as "Queen Bess," the first African American woman and the first Native American to be licensed as a pilot in 1921; the fearless Pancho Barnes, who was the first woman stunt pilot in Hollywood; and Louise Thaden, who won the first Women's Air Derby, the so-called "Powder Puff" derby, in 1929. And there are many more.

On November 2, 1929, twenty-six women pilots gathered at Curtiss Field in Valley Stream, New York, to form an international organization to promote women pilots. They called themselves the "Ninety-Nines" after the number of charter members. In 1931 they elected one of their outstanding pilots as their first president—Amelia Earhart. By then she had already made her mark on aviation history by breaking the women's altitude record of 14,000 feet, held the women's speed record, held the women's autogyro (forerunner of the helicopter) altitude record of 18,415 feet, and was the first woman to cross the Atlantic Ocean by air.[1]

Amelia was many things besides a pilot. She studied professional photography and automobile mechanics, was a fashion designer, a nurse to soldiers returning from World War I, a teacher, and author of books, poetry, and articles for various magazines. She was a member of Zonta International, a service club of executive women with the mission of "empowering women worldwide through service and advocacy." It promotes equality, education, and an end of selling of women into slavery, child marriage, and violence toward women.

Amelia Earhart amply demonstrated all of the qualities of a true hero—moral integrity, honesty, intelligence, and vision. In taking on what was clearly a "man's world," and achieving these records, she showed her courage and bravery. A less determined person without her convictions would not have succeeded. Furthermore, she had a high moral integrity and honesty, often lacking in today's heroes. Since the U.S. president's wife, Eleanor Roosevelt, was called "The First Lady," Amelia Earhart quickly was known as "The First Lady of the Skies," and because Charles Lindbergh was nicknamed "Lucky Lindy," she was named "Lady Lindy."

A Day in Grandmother's House

One of the things that influenced Amelia profoundly was the discipline she learned during her young life in late Victorian America. She lived in an age when it was rare to ride in an automobile or talk on a telephone. The first flight in a manned airplane had not yet happened; there were no jet planes or rocket ships to the moon. One had to learn discipline, self-motivation, and needed to exert considerable effort just to maintain life.

Amelia Earhart was born on July 24, 1897, in the house of her grandparents—Amelia and Judge Alfred Otis—in Atchison, Kansas. Since her father was a railroad lawyer and traveled much of the time, Amelia and her sister, Muriel, lived with their grandparents nine months of the year throughout her youth. The grandparents' Gothic-style wooden house was built overlooking the Missouri River that flowed three hundred feet below. She spent many happy years there.

I lived several years at my grandmother Ruth Martin Tonsing's house across the street from where Amelia had lived, and I can imagine what her day was like. While my grandmother's house was larger, and had electricity, running water, and indoor plumbing, living in it in the early 1940s and 1950s was similar in many ways to Amelia's life in her grandparents' house at the beginning of the twentieth century.

Young Amelia would awaken when the sun rising in the east over the distant bluffs hit the windows of her upstairs bedroom. Amelia would sit up, rub the sleep from her eyes, stretch, put on her soft slippers—the hardwood floors were cold—and then go over to a small cabinet, called a commode, which contained a pitcher of water and a deep, ceramic bowl, to wash herself. There was no indoor plumbing when Amelia was born, so the water had to be drawn up from the cistern or well outside on the south side of the house the day before, poured into the pitcher, and carried up to her bedroom.

There were no in-home bathrooms in 1900, so everything was done right in her room. In the commode was a chamber pot Amelia could use as a toilet, or she could wait until she got downstairs and go out the kitchen door to the outhouse. Outhouses had no heat, and sometimes there were spiders and even snakes in them, so they were scary places. But, when "nature" called, one had to use them. It wasn't until around 1910 or 1915 that finer homes in the East began to have rooms designated as a bathroom with indoor plumbing with a sink and toilet. I don't know when this innovation reached Kansas, but I am sure that Amy and Alfred Otis would have been the first in Atchison to install a bathroom in their house.

But before this, the chamber pot had to be carried down and taken to the outhouse and dumped each morning. Then it had to be rinsed, taken back, and placed in the commode in the bedroom. In her room, Amelia would brush her hair and tie her blond locks together with a ribbon, get dressed, and then go downstairs and through the hall back to the kitchen for breakfast. Her food would be waiting on the table.

At first, wood was burned in the cast-iron "cook" stove, but later, coal was brought to Atchison from mines in southeast Kansas. When a three-foot-thick bed of coal 1,126 feet deep was found near Atchison, it was readily available and replaced wood as fuel. The houses in Atchison then had coal bins in their basements. Monthly a coal wagon would pull up alongside the house and chunks of coal would tumble down the chute into the bin, thundering and causing the house to shake. Daily, someone would have to go down the basement steps to the bin and scoop coal into a special bucket, then carry it up to the kitchen and the fireplaces in the house.

What did Amelia eat for this first meal of the day? Oatmeal, of course. It was made from rolled oats, water, milk, and a pinch of salt, and was a staple in every household. Sometimes there would be ham, bacon, eggs, potatoes, some fruit, perhaps toast and delicious marmalade, and, of course, a glass of milk.

SCHOOL

After breakfast, Amelia would dash back upstairs, grab her books and homework, and head off to school. Grandmother Tonsing's children went to the public school. Amelia and her sister, Muriel, however, were home-schooled by a governess at first, and then went to the College Preparatory School at 304 Laramie St. a few blocks northwest of the Otis home. The school was under the direction of Helen Scofield, who remembered Amelia as "an enthusiastic child; in love with life."

What was school like for Amelia? Perhaps she arrived at the playground early so she could see her friends. When it was time for class to begin, the teacher would come out on the porch and ring a handbell—this was before electric bells or public address systems. The students would crowd through the door and head to the long, narrow cloakroom where they hung their outdoors clothes—coats, hats, earmuffs, gloves, and scarves. There were shelves above the hooks on which to put other items such as lunch boxes. It was a dark, somewhat menacing room with only a single window at the end. If a student misbehaved, hadn't done the homework, or was inattentive, the teacher would punish the student by pronouncing those dreaded words: "Go to the cloakroom!" With that, the offending student would rise slowly from the desk, walk up the aisle between sneering students to the teacher's desk and then go into the cloakroom. The student would have to stand—there were no chairs—until the teacher allowed the student to return to the classroom. One didn't know how long that would be, since it depended upon the judgment of the teacher and the severity of one's offense. I don't know whether Amelia was ever required to go to the cloakroom, but I suspect that she was not entirely unfamiliar with it.

When students entered the classroom, they went directly to their assigned desks. There they would sit on a bench, place their books on the sloping top, and sit still with their hands folded until called upon by the teacher. The teacher would stand at the front of the room behind a desk and check their names off in a grade book.

The classroom had dark wainscoting surrounding the room. On one wall was a large map of the world and on the other a framed print of the Declaration of Independence. Pictures of George Washington and Abraham Lincoln hung in frames above the blackboard.

The blackboard extended across the wall behind the teacher. A narrow shelf held white chalk and erasers. As the teacher wiped the board with the eraser, chalk dust would waft into the air. (I remember one of my teachers would wipe the board, put the chalk on the shelf, and then wipe her hands on her dress. She would go through the day with chalk handprints on her dress. We thought that was very funny.)

After roll call, the teacher would ask the class to take pencils to take a test. After the test they would copy the new spelling words and memorize them. Instead of a test, sometimes they would engage in a spelling bee.

Along with reading, these activities helped Amelia build her large vocabulary. As a result, Amelia became an author, writing articles, editorials, and columns for many newspapers and magazines. For a while it seemed as if every issue of *Reader's Digest* had an article penned by her. Amelia was the aviation editor for *Cosmopolitan* magazine and wrote articles for *National Geographic*. She also wrote books: *The Fun of It* in 1932 told about her love of flying, and *20 Hours and 40 Minutes* related her experience as a passenger on the first flight over the Atlantic Ocean by a woman. Her book, *Last Flight*, chronicled her flight around the world, which she wrote by dictating via telephone to her husband, G.P., as she traveled from California to Brazil, Africa, Pakistan, India, and New Guinea.

Students studied reading, writing, mathematics, and geography. In the early 1900s, the mind was thought to be like a muscle, and like muscles, it had to be exercised to grow. Thus, students were required to practice a lot. Amelia's instructor probably had her do the handwriting exercises in *Kittle's Penmanship* and *The Palmer Method of Writing*. Students had to fill pages and pages with circles, curls, ovals, and other shapes to perfect their cursive so it would be legible as well as beautiful. I'm sure that they were closely supervised. They had to hold the pen exactly—with the tips of the thumb, first and second fingers—and keep their wrists loose so they could flex as they wrote.

The penmanship books students used at the beginning of the twentieth century were arranged in orders of difficulty. The first book required them to copy, over and over, letters that needed only four or fewer strokes. Then they learned how to write the tall letters, and then the numbers. They would learn all the lowercase letters, then the capital letters of the alphabet, and then start writing sentences or wise sayings for practice. Amelia's handwriting shows the loops and curves learned, no doubt, from hours of penmanship practice.

Geography was an important subject in school. The students would watch as the teacher pointed out the continents, countries, major cities, rivers, mountain ranges, and deserts. They would learn about the resources there, how the people dressed, what they ate, and how they lived. They were taught about the oceans, the currents, the larger islands, and about weather phenomena like typhoons, hurricanes, and monsoons. When Amelia made her last flight around the world, she already knew a lot about the countries she visited, putting to good use the lessons she learned in school.

For many schoolchildren, recess was the high point of the day. The girls often would play hopscotch, jump rope, or tag. But Amelia also was attracted to high-energy games like dodgeball, kickball, or softball. It was thought in that day that these activities were important to "warm up the brain for better learning."

Most of all, Amelia's teachers instilled a love of reading in the girl. She liked to come over to Grandmother Tonsing's house and choose a book from the large library there. When my great-grandparents, Col. John A. and Ida Challiss Martin, built the house in 1871, it contained not only a parlor but a large library, about half the size of the fourteen-room house, that held over 6,000 books, the largest library, public or private, in the state of Kansas at the time. I don't know what books Amelia chose to read, but I imagine they were adventure stories as well as books about travel.

AFTER-SCHOOL CHORES

When Amelia arrived home she never went into the yard

by going through the gate. She loved to hop over the fence instead, much to her grandmother's horror. Little women were supposed to walk and not run, and certainly not leap over fences. After a day at school, Amelia was ready to play. Before she could do so, however, she had to do chores. This was something expected of all children. For Amelia it was to sweep floors, dust furniture, pull weeds, or rake leaves. After Melville Bissell invented the carpet sweeper in 1876, cleaning the rugs in the house was easier. But to get the smaller rugs clean, they were rolled up, taken outside, and hung on a line in order to thump them with a carpet beater, a long handle with a flat paddle either of wire or cane. I imagine that once Amelia got into it, she had fun whacking the rug with all of her might to see the dust fly up in a cloud.

In the days before electricity, homes were lighted with kerosene or oil lamps. Oil was cleaner, but kerosene burned brighter. The lamps usually consisted of a round, glass body that held the oil, a brass burner with tines to hold the chimney upright, a flat, cotton wick, and a glass chimney. Capillary action in the wick drew the kerosene up from the fuel reservoir and the flame would be fed air coming up from the sides of the burner.

The lamps gave a warm glow to the rooms at night, and could be adjusted brighter or softer with a round knob at the side of the burner. After each evening's use, the chimney had to be cleaned of the black soot that collected in it. This was done by draping a cloth over a long, wooden spoon which was rubbed around and around until all of the soot was gone. This was a chore that had to be done each day.

While Amelia's grandparents usually had a maid to do the cooking and the major cleaning, it is not unlikely that Amelia helped with the weekly washing of clothes. The dirty clothes were brought downstairs in baskets and carried outdoors to the south side of the house or downstairs to the washroom facing the alley. Water was drawn from the well to fill three copper tubs. Fires were lit under two of these tubs to heat the water. In the first tub, flakes of Oxydol, Lux, or Star Naphtha Washing Powder were poured into the water. If they didn't use any of these commercial soap products, flakes were carved with a knife from a dark-brown bar of Fels-Naptha soap.

Since this was before electric-powered washing machines, a long, wooden paddle was used to stir up the soap. When the water was boiling, the clothes were put in and agitated with a "dollie," a rod with two handles at the top, and a round base with four wooden pegs extending from the bottom that looked like a little stool. Another type of agitator was a rod with an upside-down, perforated, tin funnel that would be moved up and down in the tub. Such a job would have been ideal for a young girl like Amelia.

When the clothes were "done," they would be twisted by hand or squeezed between two rubber rollers turned with a crank into the second tub of hot water to rinse them. They would be stirred again, rung out and put into the third tank of cold water. Finally, they would be rung, placed into a basket, and hung with wooden clothespins on a clothesline. When all of the clothes were hung, I can imagine Amelia and Muriel running up and down the lines of wind-blown sheets to play hide-and-seek since it was so much fun.

As the clothes were drying, Amelia was assigned to look out of the windows of the house frequently to see if any rain clouds were approaching. If they were, I can imagine that she alerted everyone. They would rush outside, take down the clothes, and hurry inside with them before the raindrops fell.

After the clothes were dry, they had to be taken down and put into baskets and the clothespins put back into the cloth sack. The baskets were taken inside where the clothes were separated. Some were to be folded and taken to the cupboard or chest-of-drawers upstairs. Amelia would be enlisted to help iron the clothes too. This was a hot, difficult job. The ironing board would be taken out of the closet and set up in the kitchen. Before electric steam irons, two, heavy metal "flat irons" (also called "sad" irons after an old word for "solid") were heated on the kitchen stove. The irons could not be heated too much though, since they might scorch the clothing. The temperature was tested by wetting a finger and touching it to the iron surface to see if it would sizzle and steam. It was important to keep the irons clean and polished. Sometimes they would have to be sand-papered and then wiped with grease or beeswax so that they would glide easily over the cloth.

While one iron heated on the stove, the other was used to smooth out the wrinkles in the sheets and clothes. If the clothes were too dry, the cloth was sprinkled with water. When the cloth had to be shifted on the ironing board or changed, the iron was placed on a trivet shaped like the bottom of the iron. When one iron got cool, it was swapped with the hot one and reheated until all of the laundry was pressed.

Saturdays were for the weekly chore of polishing the silver. This included not only the eating utensils, but also serving plates, salt and pepper cellars, coffee pot, teapot, sugar bowl, cream pitcher, candlesticks, silver flower vase, or fruit compote for the dining table.

If the silverware was tarnished, however, the pieces were placed on the kitchen table to be polished. Various solutions were used to polish the silver. In Amelia's days, a runny paste of chalk ("whiting"), alum, or cream of tartar was picked up by a piece of cloth on the tip of a finger and gently rubbed on the silver. An old, worn-out toothbrush was used to get into the cracks until it shined. After an inspection by grandmother or the maid, the silver was washed again in clean water and gently dried with a soft cloth, and the items finally could be placed back in the drawer or cupboard. It was a good, rainy-day job to keep children's hands busy when they couldn't go outside to play. I can't imagine that Amelia liked to do it, however.

Amelia learned discipline and hard work through these chores. I know that in later years, Amelia enjoyed working on her airplane engines. She was interested in mechanics and took an automobile repair course in high school to learn how machines worked. Amelia probably thought the difficult, dirty work of repairing an airplane engine was far less onerous than having to do chores at home, but she also learned that when things needed to be done, one does them to the best of one's ability and doesn't complain.

After completing her chores, Amelia probably couldn't wait to run out to play with her sister and her cousins — Lucy Challiss, who lived just south of the Otis house, and Orpha Tonsing—and perhaps her brothers, Evan and little Bob Tonsing—who lived just north of her. There was no end to what the kids did together. My Aunt Orpha was the same age as Amelia. She said Amelia was always the ringleader in their games, organizing the other kids in their play, was very athletic, and did everything with a lot of energy.

Sunday mornings were reserved for church, so Saturday night was for taking a bath in order to be clean and nice for the next day. There were no showers or bathrooms in Victorian houses of the early 1900s, so a copper or tin tub was dragged into the middle of the kitchen. It had a flat bottom and slightly flaring sides. One round end was higher than the other so that one could lean back in it. Water was drawn from the well or cistern outside and carried in, heated on the kitchen stove, and poured into the tub. Since the tub was metal, even the rim became quite hot. A stool with a towel and a bar of soap was placed nearby. Everyone in the family, starting with the oldest to the youngest, would take a bath in the same water. The first ones to bathe had warm water, but by the last, the water was cold, even though a little more hot water was poured into the tub from the stove for each bath. After everyone was scrubbed and clean, the tub was emptied, wiped out with a towel, and dragged back behind the stove to await next Saturday's baths.

Sundays

Sunday morning came, and Amelia would get up, dress, and go down to the kitchen. After breakfast, Amelia would return to her room to change into her "good, going-to-church clothes." Her grandfather would hitch the horse to the carriage, and the family would climb into the carriage for the ride to Trinity Episcopal Church.

Judge Alfred Otis was an elder at the church, and the family always sat in front. When they walked down the central aisle to their seats, Amelia would walk behind them, but always energetically, sometimes on her toes and sometimes skipping down the aisle. After the service and visiting with friends, the family returned home for a formal Sunday dinner. The dining table was covered with a tablecloth and carefully folded linen napkins, silverware, and fresh flowers from Grandmother Otis' garden.

Grandmother's garden provided vegetables such as string beans, peas, tomatoes, cucumbers, carrots, turnips, onions, and potatoes. Others she didn't grow were delivered weekly, along with milk and meat. Since there was no electricity and no refrigerators in houses at that time, the only way to keep the produce from spoiling was to take it downstairs to the basement root cellar, a rectangular hole in the earth that was covered with a wooden lid.

For items like milk, that had to be kept cooler, there was an insulated icebox. Each week, a wagon would pull up alongside the house and a burly man would take metal tongs and swing a block of ice up onto his shoulders, which were covered with a leather cape, bring it into the kitchen, and put it in the top of the icebox. The ice would keep the food below it cool. The ice would gradually melt during the week, however, so each morning, the first thing one had to do when in the kitchen was to reach under the icebox and pull out the drip pan (or catch tray) and empty it into the sink. Otherwise, water would flow over the floor and get everything wet.

Amelia and her sister had to sit properly to eat dinner, observing the manners she had learned from her grandmother—using the proper utensil and in the correct order, passing the platters of food from the right to the left, not talking with the mouth full, and keeping elbows off of the table. There would be roast beef or pork, potatoes and gravy, along with the vegetables. There was no question about refusing to eat something; it was to be eaten whether one liked it or not. There also would be fresh baked buns with butter and some marmalade. Finally, there would be delicious desserts—cakes, pies, and, especially, ice cream. Amelia encountered all sorts of strange foods in her travels around the world, and, out of politeness, she probably seldom complained or refused to eat them. She always wanted to be gracious to her hosts.

Amelia also learned how to conduct well-mannered conversation around the dining table. She and her sister would likely be asked questions about what they had learned in school and what they knew about many topics. Throughout her adult life, Amelia was a much-sought guest by kings and queens of Europe, President Franklin and Eleanor Roosevelt in Washington, D.C., and William Randolph Hearst in his "castle" on the central California coast. She charmed them with her conversation, her knowledge, and her personality.

THE PARLOR

There was one room in the house that was forbidden to children except when they were invited into it on special occasions, or during cold winter nights. It was called the "sitting room" or parlor, which was on the southeast corner of the house. When Amelia and Muriel were invited to join the grown-ups, they had to sit erect on their chairs, with their hands folded on their laps. The rule then was that "Children are meant to be seen and not heard!" That is, children could speak only when spoken to. I can imagine Amelia sitting there very quietly on the outside while nearly bursting with something she wanted to say. Here, Amelia learned how to conduct "polite" and respectful conversations that enabled her to plan and negotiate her trips with the many individuals who made up her "teams" for her flights.

Midway between dinner at noon and the late supper in the evening, Amy Otis would serve tea, as was the custom. There would be little sandwiches, cookies, and some "sweets."

The tea served to the little girls was much watered down. Amelia learned a lot from her grandmother about how to behave, how to hold a cup and saucer, to dab her napkin on her mouth and not swipe it across, and to ask politely for more and not grab the teapot. The skills she learned at the tea table enabled her to enjoy having tea and dining with the leaders of the nations here and abroad.

After supper during the summer, the family would relax on the porch facing the river with Amelia and Muriel dashing around the yard catching fireflies as they lit the night with streaks of light flashing from their tails. They would cup them in their hands and peek through their fingers to watch the little bugs turn on and off, or put them into glass Mason jars to study. If it was very hot, the downstairs windows were opened to let in the cool air, and the windows upstairs would be opened wide. The air would be drawn in and up the stairs and out through the windows, the house acting as a large chimney.

In winter, the house was never warm enough, so the family would gather around the fireplace in the parlor where it was cozy. While the family was eating supper, the maid would shut the doors to the entrance hallway and close the pocket doors that led from the parlor to the library. Then the maid would light the fireplace so that the room would be nice and "toasty" by the time the family came into the parlor for the evening. Family members and sometimes guests talked or read by the light of the fireplace and oil lamps. It was a time to dream of faraway places, and imagine what it would be like to go there. This was long before Amelia was able to take to the air and visit these exotic lands herself, but it laid the groundwork for her future trips.

Finally, when her eyelids drooped and she became sleepy, Amelia would go upstairs to her bedroom, put on her nightgown, and curl up in bed. Since there was no furnace in the house, when it was cold, her grandmother would heat bricks on the kitchen stove after supper. Then she would wrap them in a towel or newspapers and put them under the covers at the foot of Amelia's bed, keeping it warm until morning.

This was the world in which Amelia Earhart grew up. It was very different from our own. Whenever she and her cousins played in the Otis, Challiss, or Tonsing yards, or the families gathered for special occasions, or joined together for a meal, they enjoyed one another and bonded. Amelia was beloved by her relatives, and when she crashed into the Pacific Ocean in 1937, the family grieved profoundly; they had lost a wonderful member of the family, one who was cherished by all of them.

Chapter Two

COUSIN AMELIA

Statue of Amelia Earhart by Ernst Shelton,
North Hollywood, California
Photograph by Ernst F. Tonsing

Everyone who knew Amelia Earhart when she was a child agreed that she was energetic, resourceful, extremely brave, and a natural leader. They were not surprised to see her go on to accomplish astonishing feats as an adult. Atchison, Kansas, was just the place to be born for an adventurous girl like Amelia in 1897. The spirit of doing something no one else had done before, of pushing out into the unknown, and of seeking excitement, was part of the fabric of the town at that time. Located on the "Great Western Bend" of the Missouri River where the turbulent waterway extended in a giant arc some fifteen miles farther west than at any other place on the Missouri and Kansas border, the town was perched on two nearly three-hundred-foot high plateaus of Oread Limestone on either side of the unruly White Clay Creek.[2]

The famed explorers Captains William Clark and Meriwether Lewis stopped at White Clay Creek in what is now downtown Atchison on their way to explore the newly acquired Louisiana Purchase. They had been sent by President Thomas Jefferson to investigate rumors of giant bones and tusks found in the rocks and huge, hairy, horned beasts that roamed there in the millions. They stopped where the creek empties into the Missouri River. After looking around a bit, they proceeded up the river to another stream, which they named Fourth of July Creek. There they camped and celebrated the holiday at sunset by firing a cannon they had brought with them. The next day they headed out into the unknown—the Great Plains, the Dakotas, the Rocky Mountains, and as far west as the mouth of the Columbia River in Oregon—the very edge of the continent itself.

Fifty years later in 1853, there were only about ten small settlements in all of Kansas plus some trading posts and missions. In May 1854, when Congress passed the Kansas-Nebraska Act and Kansas was made a U.S. territory, settlers began to arrive. Dr. John H. Stringfellow and several others struck out from Platte City, Missouri, to find a new place to live. Arriving in the Atchison area, they found a "squatter," George M. Million, living in his log hut by the river at the foot of what later became Atchison Street, and another, whose name was Samuel Dickson, who had a nearby claim. Stringfellow bargained with the squatters and obtained their claims for the huge sum of $1,000.[3]

A week later, alongside the river and below the future site of the house in which Amelia was born forty-three years later, "under the shade of some time-honored and sturdy old giants of the forest," Stringfellow, P.T. Abell, J.N. Barnes, along with eleven others, organized the Atchison Town Company.[4] It was named in honor of a U.S. senator from Missouri, the fire-breathing, pro-slavery, David Rice Atchison. Their purpose was to ensure that when the territory was admitted into the union, Kansas would be a slave state.

Lots were sold, buildings erected, and soon merchants and settlers came to live there. On April 10, 1855, the U.S. Post Office designated Atchison as the headquarters for mail going west. By 1856, there were fifty new buildings. Dr. William L. Challiss, the husband of Amelia's great-aunt Mary Ann, purchased Million's little ferry that crossed the river from Missouri to the levee at Atchison Street, and then brought a larger one from the east when the traffic increased. His brother, George T. Challiss, erected the first general merchandise store at the northeast corner of Commercial and the levee anticipating that great numbers of immigrants would be passing through Atchison.[5]

Schools, academies, churches, and hotels were constructed. Soon not only settlers but prospectors, merchants, and farmers crossed the Missouri on William Challiss' ferry, purchased provisions for their journey at George Challiss' store, and then headed out across the prairies to distant Colorado, Utah, California, and Oregon.

Not only was Atchison the place of departure for countless pioneers but also for wagons laden with merchandise. In 1865, alone, there were 4,917 wagons, with 6,164 mules, 27,685 oxen, and 1,256 men, rumbling through town heading for the gold mines in Colorado, to Salt Lake City, and the forests of the Northwest coast.[6] One can imagine wide-eyed Amelia and her sister, Muriel, listening to her grandmother tell of the mile-long trains of "white canvas wagons" being driven by men with "long, hairy, grizzly beards," creating the "powerful music" of the bullwhacker's whips over oxen as they left Atchison for the six-week trip to Denver.[7]

On the levee, at the foot of what is now Commercial Street, stood a large elm tree. This was the starting place for the Butterfield Overland Stage Line heading west from Atchison.[8] Besides mail, it charged $75 a passenger for the five- or six-day ride to Denver, and $300 for the eighteen-day journey to Placerville and the gold mines in California.[9]

For many years, steamboats and stagecoaches were the only means of travel to Atchison, and news and newspapers were a week old by the time they arrived.[10] In the 1850s and '60s, Atchison became a shipping point for farmers and traders wishing to send their wheat or pelts east.[11] When President Abraham Lincoln signed the Homestead Act on May 20, 1862, where a person could pay a small fee and obtain 160 acres of land, provided that it was continuously occupied and improved over five years, it brought a bonus to Atchison. Now thousands of pioneers passed through the town needing more goods to supply them.

Efficient and fast transportation was increasingly necessary. Led by Cyrus K. Holliday and Amelia's great-uncle, Luther C. Challiss, a lawyer and brother to George and William Challiss, a new railroad was formally organized September 15-17, 1860, in Challiss' law office. The Civil War and droughts delayed their attempts to get it going, however. Meanwhile, the Central Branch Railroad was incorporated by the Kansas Territorial Legislature in 1859 and ran west one hundred miles from Atchison to Waterville, and the Atchison & Nebraska Railroad began in 1868, going north to Lincoln, Nebraska.[12]

Finally, construction began on Holliday's and Luther Challiss' Santa Fe railroad , and the company became one of the largest in the United States. Amelia would have heard the whistles of these trains as they crossed the 1875 bridge over the Missouri and rumbled through town. Too bad she never knew the song Judy Garland sang about that railroad in the 1946 movie, *The Harvey Girls*. She would have loved to sing:

Do you hear that whistle down the line?
I figure that it's Engine Number 49
She's the only one that'll sound that way,
On the Atchison, Topeka & the Santa Fe.[13]

We can imagine Amelia's mother and other relatives telling her of their early days in Atchison, of the twisting road that ran alongside what was later Commercial Street, the narrow, rickety wooden bridge over the treacherous White

Clay Creek, and of the large frog pond between Sixth and Seventh streets north of Commercial in which the young people used to fish in summers and skate on the ice in winters.[14] Amelia must have smiled when she thought of the children of old Atchison, especially the daring glides, arabesques, and spins they did on skates on the frozen pond.

Amelia's family and the Challiss, Otis, and Martin families came to Atchison in the 1850s and purchased lots on First (later Terrace) Street high on the bluffs of the Missouri River. This became almost a family enclave. Amelia's grandparents, Amelia Josephine Harres, and Judge Alfred Otis, built a frame house at 223 N. Terrace St. South of this house was the home of her aunt and uncle, Mary Ann and Dr. William L. Challiss, and their ten children.[15] Located on what was called Challiss Point, the three-story house with its twin chimneys, verandas, and tall, round, pointed turret, was an imposing building that could be seen far to the south and the north from the boats going by on the Missouri River. The furnishings in the house were of the latest and finest quality that could be shipped from the East.

A hundred yards north was the house of cousin Ida Challiss Martin, the widow of former Kansas governor, John Alexander Martin.[16] Built in 1871, it also was the home of her daughter, Ruth, her husband, Paul Gerhardt Tonsing, and their seven children,[17] (among them my father, Ernest Frederick Tonsing). Amelia and her sister were playmates of my older aunts and uncles and occasionally babysitters for my father and his twin sister, Ida.

Amelia was born July 24, 1897, in the sunny, southwest room of her maternal grandparents' Otis' home.[18] Amy Otis Earhart had gone there to be with her parents during her "period of confinement," which was not unusual at that time. Amy already had lost a child who had been stillborn in August 1896, and it was thought necessary to take this precaution. Baby Amelia was named Amelia Mary Earhart, after the custom of combining the name of her maternal grandmother, Amelia Josephine Harres, and her paternal grandmother, Mary Wells Patton Earhart.[19] Shortly after she was born, Amelia was baptized at Trinity Episcopal Church where her grandparents were prominent members and generous donors.[20]

Amelia was nicknamed "Meeley" (or "Millie") as a child. Her sister, Muriel Grace, was born two years later, in 1899, and was nicknamed "Pidge."[21] Family members called the girls by their nicknames well into adulthood.

The Otis house had a large, iron statue of a dog in front, which Amelia and Muriel liked to ride "like a pony."[22] The house was surrounded by a white picket fence then, with a gate and tall, sturdy gateposts in the front. The two girls liked to sit on top of these posts to look out and down the thickly overgrown banks to the Missouri River, some three hundred feet below. From up there they could study the swirls of the currents and watch the government snag boats pulling sunken logs out of the water so that the riverboats could navigate safely. Even more exciting was to watch the Atchison Bridge twist on its axis to allow the riverboats to pass through on their way up and down the river.

My cousins, uncles, and aunts all agreed that from her youth, Amelia always wanted to go faster and farther in whatever apparatus was available. She built a ramp from the roof of the toolshed behind the house and cascaded down it in a wooden box. She spilled out of it at the bottom, tore her dress, and bruised her lip, but was ecstatic about the ride. All the Earhart, Challiss, and Tonsing children enjoyed rattling down the red brick Terrace Street or Santa Fe Street in various contraptions. Wheels were attached to boxes and boards and then pushed or dragged along the streets. Amelia also loved to sled in winter. While the boys could do "belly-flops" and ride sleds prone, it was only proper for young ladies to sit upright on the sled. Not so for Amelia; she would belly-flop with the boys and try to beat them downhill on the sled.

A block west of her grandparents' house is Second Street. It is a steep hill going downtown from the bluff on which her house sat, and was a favorite sledding hill. Once when Amelia was hurtling down this hill, a horse and wagon started across the street close to the bottom. Completely unfazed, Amelia steered the sled right under the belly of the horse, avoiding the legs and wheels. When she reached the bottom she started jumping around and shouting to her sister who stood at the top of the hill: "Yippie! Yippie! That was just like flying!"

Amelia liked to visit the Tonsing house to play. Grandmother Tonsing and my Aunt Ida told me that no clock was safe in the house when Amelia was there. She would have the clock off the shelf and taken apart "in a jiffy," as my grandmother told it. Amelia would sit on the floor with the clock parts all around her. She would pick up each piece and study it to see how it worked in the timepiece. My grandmother also said Amelia would put the clock back together and have it running just as quickly.[23] She just loved to figure out how things worked.

My grandmother also told me that Amelia loved the swing on the front porch. The swing was wide, able to hold three adults or a number of children. It was made of thin, round slats and the front and back curled gracefully. Amelia would get the swing going higher and higher so that she could almost touch the ceiling of the porch. That alarmed my grandmother, and she would have to tell Amelia not to go so high since she was afraid that the grommets that held the chains to the ceiling would pull out and dump Amelia either on the porch or the lawn.

Amelia also liked to babysit. My cousin, Beatsie Challiss Laws, recalled that Amelia would take my father, Ernest, and his twin sister, Ida, out for a stroll in the perambulator—that's what they called a baby buggy in those days—and run so fast with it that my grandmother would have to come out and tell Amelia to slow down; my grandmother was afraid the babies would go flying out of the buggy and on to the ground.

Wandering through the jungle-like bushes and trees on the steep slopes of the riverbanks and exploring the caves in the cliffs was always a temptation. The Tonsings' youngest son, Paul Martin Tonsing (called Junior), was born too late to be included in the play with the Earhart girls.[24] He told me it was always forbidden for the children to enter the caves in the cliffs, but, of course, that didn't stop any of them from exploring and finding all sorts of interesting things in them. The caves were shallow, just enough to hang out and pretend they were robbers hiding from the sheriff or shielding themselves from some terrifying beast. The children, however, would never mention to their parents that they had gone into the caves.

Sometimes they would see real beasts there—squirrels, weird possums, fast foxes, and even an occasional bashful deer. What Amelia didn't want to see were the cute, black kittens that had two white stripes down their backs—otherwise known as skunks. As she walked along the top of the bluffs, Amelia encountered other animals—grouse, prairie-chickens, ring-necked pheasants, or even wild turkeys. At night, Amelia would hear the whippoorwills and the nighthawks calling to one another in the darkness. When she climbed down the steep brush and tree-covered slopes to the river below, she would see blue herons, snowy egrets, blue jays, and American crows. Swallows darted around gathering water and mud to build their little nests in the eves of the barn. In the winter, the bright, red cardinals would come, pecking in the snow for seeds. In the barn, Amelia would see barn owls, with their large heads and white, heart-shaped faces. Occasionally, she would hear screech owls.

Most of all, I imagine, Amelia was fascinated by the red-shouldered hawks, the gray hawks, and others, sailing out over the river on their outstretched wings, gliding and catching the wind currents to rise higher and higher. I wonder whether Amelia ever dreamed of flying then, or ever imagined that she would join these birds in the air and fly from coast to coast and continent to continent.

When she saw her first airplane at the age of ten at the Iowa State Fair in Des Moines, perhaps Amelia thought of these birds, gliding through the air. At the time, however, Amelia said she wasn't sure she wanted to go up into one of those rickety biplanes made of "rusty wire and wood." She was much more interested in the merry-go-round.

My father's oldest sister, Orpah Tonsing,[24] said since all of the cousins—the Challiss, Tonsing and Earhart children—lived so close to one another, they played together in Mrs. Otis' rose garden. It was said to be one of the most beautiful in town—just south of their home (a house stands there now). Orpah related:

I often played with Amelia and Muriel after school when they lived with or visited their grandparents. I remember all the toys in the area under the stairway— stone blocks, Jack Straws, and the big bisque doll in the nice carriage. One had a face of cloth, painted so beautifully. I was at this time living in the Challiss house, next to the Otises, since my great-grandparents had moved to Adrian, Michigan.

The Martins still lived in their home. The Otises frequently invited me to Sunday dinner. I think they missed their granddaughters. When Grandma Ida [Martin] moved away, we moved to the Martin home, where I grew to ladyhood.[25]

Amelia and Muriel spent a lot of time playing in the old Otis barn across the street. Charlie Parks, the houseman for the Otis family, built dollhouses in the barn for the children, and cousin Jack Challiss devised all sorts of games for them to play, some of them rather rambunctious, I was told. Yet, the Earhart girls were certainly well-disciplined by their grandmother, Amelia Otis. They had formal little tea parties on the lawn in front of the house, and learned to sit properly with their family's friends in the parlor of the house and carry on "adult" conversations.

My Aunt Orpah thought Amelia's spirit was irrepressible. Members of Trinity Episcopal Church agreed:

They remember seeing Amelia Earhart following her grandparents, devout members of the church, down the aisle of the church to their pew near the front. Amelia, small and wiry, walked as though on air. She was always intensely alive.[26]

The photographs of Amelia are usually in black and white, but one can see that her hair was light. In fact, it was very blond. When she had her hair cut, shortly before her last flight, the barber kept a lock of her hair, which is preserved at the Atchison Birthplace Museum.

At times, the girls played hard and even got "scuffled up" and dirty. Finally, Amy had them get out of their dresses and wear bloomers to play. These originally were called Turkish dresses and came to be popular in America during the mid-nineteenth century. They gave the young girls the ability to move freely and would not restrict their play.

Not everyone approved of the bloomers, however, my grandmother included. While grandmother didn't mind the energetic antics of her neighbor's children, as she had many of her own in the yard mingling with them, I remember that on several occasions grandmother said she didn't think it quite proper for Amelia and her sister to be so oddly dressed as young women.

There was another reason for her disapproval. Named after Amelia Jenks Bloomer, who reformed women's manner of dress by wearing loose trousers gathered at the ankles, women began wearing the pants-like costume from the 1850s as a sign of their support for women's rights and suffrage.[27] Bloomers were adopted by prominent women activists of the era, especially abolitionist and suffragist Lucy Stone, who wore bloomers when she spoke to big crowds. Thus, at the beginning of the twentieth century, when Amy Earhart dressed her daughters in bloomers, anyone who saw these children dressed this way also would recognize it as a political statement.

Grandmother Ruth Tonsing was certainly not against women's right to vote and progress for women in the work-

Ernst F. Tonsing

force and politics, nor was her mother, Ida Challiss Martin. According to her diary, Ida Martin entertained prominent women in the suffrage movement and was behind her husband's signing the bill permitting women to vote in Kansas municipal elections in 1887 when he was governor of the state. This was many years before the ratification of the Nineteenth Amendment in 1920.[28] Ruth Tonsing was an eager patriot and voter, but she said it offended her rather Victorian sense of propriety when she saw her cousin and neighbor permitting their daughters to dress in bloomers. Amelia and Muriel loved them, however, since they gave them the freedom to play as hard as they wanted.

Chapter Three

THE BRAVE
GREAT-GRANDMOTHER
MARIA GRACE HARRES

Maria Grace Harres, ca. 1860

Ernst F. Tonsing

Growing up at the turn of the century in Atchison, Kansas, left its mark on Amelia Earhart, but as important was the influence of her remarkable family. Members of the Harres, Challiss, Martin, Earhart, and Otis families were positive role models, providing fine examples of how one confronts life's challenges. Directly or indirectly, they inspired the confidence for Amelia to achieve her goals. They demonstrated the ability to overcome great obstacles and inspired others with their passion, living lives of service, working hard to direct their skills and intelligence toward a common good with no trace of arrogance.

Amelia's mother, Amy Earhart, wrote a letter to her cousin Ruth Martin Tonsing on April 8, 1942, revealing that Amelia's ancestors were as remarkable and adventurous as she was. The four-page document was typed, single-spaced, and every bit of the pages were filled, even to the margins and bottom.[29] In it she recalled that her grandfather, Gebhard Harres was one of the prominent businessmen of Philadelphia. Gebhard was born June 11, 1801, or 1802, in Valstadt, Braunschweig, Niedersachsen (Brunswick, Lower Saxony), Germany, a city that was a member of the Hanseatic League from the thirteenth to the middle of the seventeenth centuries, and was known for its hams and sausages. Since Gebhard disliked farmwork, he had been apprenticed to a cabinetmaker, making furniture.[30]

The Napoleonic Wars were raging in Europe, and prior to the Battle of Quatre Bras on June 18, 1815, and the Battle of Waterloo on June 18, 1815, officers were going into every town and village to conscript soldiers to fight against the French emperor.[31] Gebhard had four brothers who had been caught in the field where they were working and drafted into the army. Gebhard's parents were determined that they were not going to let this happen to him, so they sent him secretly to America.[32] They gave him what money they had, and his mother wrapped up the slate he had used for his schoolwork,[33] an extra shirt, wool hose, and he took off.[34] Gebhard traveled nine days, running by night and hiding during the day.

Finally, he made it to the Netherlands, 125 miles away, traveling part of the way in a wagon beneath a cargo of strong-smelling cheeses. He then signed on as a seaman aboard a Dutch ship that he thought would take him to the United States. But it went to the wrong America—instead, traveling to South America. Once more he boarded an American ship, expecting it to sail to the United States, but it took him to England with a cargo of fruit and sugar, and then to the West Indies in the Caribbean. It was two years before Gebhard arrived in the United States, but in the meantime he had earned some money and learned to speak excellent English by recording new words on his school slate.

At first, Gebhard worked as a toolmaker for Robert Fulton, the famous inventor of the first successful steamboat, and John Stevens, who invented the first U.S. steam locomotive and steam-powered ferry. In his spare time, Gebhard used his slate to draw diagrams of steam-powered pistons for running machines in the shops.[35] With the money he earned, Gebhard opened a cabinetmaker's shop to make fine furniture. He built up his business in Philadelphia until eventually he had forty apprentices to do most of the work.

One day, a girl several years older than he came into the shop. Maria Grace Neville (or Nevle), was born to a Quaker family in Germantown, a suburb of Philadelphia, on August 2, 1797. Her Quaker ancestors came to America with William Penn in 1682. She remembered being lifted up on her father's shoulders to see George Washington pass by on the way to open Congress when Philadelphia was the nation's capital.[36]

As a young girl, Maria Grace was chosen by the city of Philadelphia to present flowers to General Lafayette in a ceremony honoring the Revolutionary War hero when he visited the city.[37] She was married to a sea captain when she was sixteen years old, but her husband left the next day on a ship and never was seen again. This gave her a lifelong fear of the ocean and of ships.

Gebhard and Maria Grace were immediately smitten with each other and married on October 17, 1821. Since he was a Lutheran, her Quaker church disapproved of the match and her name was stricken from the records of the Society of Friends.[38]

According to Amy, Gebhard was very handsome. He stood six feet four, had rosy cheeks, blue eyes, and naturally curly hair. When dressed in his ruffled shirt, blue breeches, and shoes with silver buckles, the costume for men in his day, Amy said, "he must have made quite a picture." And Gebhard thought Maria Grace was "the most beautiful person in Philadelphia." They were such a striking couple that when people passed by, they would turn around to look at them.[39]

With the apprentices in the shop and her family to take care of, Maria Grace worked hard managing the large household. Amy speculated this may have been the reason she lost her first three babies. In time, they moved to a three-story house on lower Chestnut Street where they had seven maids to take care of the home and the family that included eight children. Maids polished the silver door knocker and scrubbed the marble steps that led up to the house each day, and the hundred twenty-five windows that looked out onto the garden were washed every week.[40]

Maria Grace also was very brave. She tirelessly nursed many friends during the cholera epidemic of 1832 that killed a thousand people just in Philadelphia. Her father was quite forward-thinking and had Maria Grace inoculated for smallpox, a hazardous thing to do at that time. Once again, she saved many friends during a subsequent smallpox epidemic. Still, according to Amy, Maria Grace did not like adventure very much.[41] Living to nearly one hundred years old, Maria Grace was vigorous and alert to the end. She was very proud to see the birth of her great-great-grandchildren—my aunt and uncle, Evan and Orpah Tonsing.

Gebhard toiled hard during the day, but after business hours, he worked in his garden, "experimenting with fruits and flowers," according to Amy. He grafted plants in various ways and was known for his grapes and pears. He was a very "kind and gentle" person, had a pet turtle, and loved to feed birds that ate out of his hand. According to Maria Grace he "spoiled her always."[42]

On June 20, 1835, after several years of marriage, Gebhard returned to Germany for a visit.[43] It was a long and dangerous trip, taking up to three months to cross the Atlantic. Luxury liners did not exist then, so he had to take his own blankets and pillow and a sizable amount of cooked food aboard the ship. When he left, Maria Grace thought she would never see him again and had the servants close the shutters on the windows of the house; she was a "tearful wreck" until he returned six months later. Gebhard arrived in Braunschweig to discover that his mother was

Ernst F. Tonsing

dead and his brothers had been killed in the war, confirming the judgment of his parents to send him to America. He made several trips after that to visit his father.[44] Maria Grace and Gebhard's children were raised in luxury. Their daughters were women of great "delicacy and good taste," according to Amy. Yet, even though she was born into one of the most aristocratic families in Philadelphia, daughter Mary Ann moved in 1857 to the very edge of civilization in the Kansas Territory where buffalo still roamed freely over the prairies and deer grazed under the branches of the oak and cottonwood trees. She had married a doctor from New Jersey—William L. Challiss—and the couple arrived in the new community of Atchison. The little town had few permanent buildings, no paved streets, and hogs rooted on the main avenue.

Mary Ann's sister, Amelia Harres, came to Atchison in 1860 as a "summer girl," intending to return to Philadelphia in the fall. In Atchison, she became acquainted with a "rising young lawyer," Alfred G. Otis. They were married shortly thereafter in Philadelphia, on April 22, 1862, and returned to Atchison to raise seven children,[45] one of whom gave birth to Amelia Earhart.

Maria Grace died September 17, 1896, in the home of daughter Amelia Harres and her husband, Alfred Otis in Atchison, Kansas. Her body was taken back to historic Laurel Hill Cemetery in Philadelphia to rest beside her husband, Gebhard. Their graves are marked by a tall obelisk.

Chapter Four

THE ADVENTUROUS GREAT-GRANDFATHER GEBHARD HARRES

Gebhard Harres, ca. 1860

Ernst F. Tonsing

melia's great-grandfather Gebhard Harres was quite an adventurer, the opposite of his cautious wife, Maria Grace. As an eminent Philadelphia businessman, Gebhard was invited in 1832 to ride on the first railroad train from the city. In the early nineteenth century, few streets in American cities were paved, and most roads became avenues of deep mud in the rain. There were some experiments in laying wood rails on cross ties to facilitate the movement of special carts, such as those used in mines, but the major problem for these "rail roads" was devising the propulsion. The cars that moved on rails at the time were pulled by horses or pushed by humans.

The early nineteenth century produced a number of inventors who worked on the problem of locomotion. A fascinating solution was the "atmospheric railway" proposed by the physicist, philosopher, and mathematician Papin, of Blois, France. The carriages would be thrust through a large tube by vacuum and air pressure. Such a train was constructed in Sydenham, England, for the Great Exposition of 1851 at the Crystal Palace. It consisted of a brick tube nine feet high and eight feet wide, and a quarter-mile in length. A steam engine exhausted as well as compressed the air to move the car. Those who were courageous enough to ride in this machine reported that "the motion of the car was pleasant, and the ventilation ample."[46]

One inventor thought the solution to propel the cars was to fit them with sails, and experiments were conducted in Holland, Spain, and China. In the United States, the most successful line of this type was operated by C.J. Bascom of the Kansas Pacific Railroad. After several years of service, a handcar was refitted with a mast eleven feet high and a triangular sail suspended between two booms. It could achieve forty miles per hour on the plains of Kansas.[47] An engraving of the "sailing car" shows the cart and its billowing sails speeding along the tracks. Two passengers lean forward in the exhilaration of the ride, one stands holding his cap while the other looks back to his hat, which had been blown off his head. Below a sky filled with turbulent clouds, a horse looks up in astonishment at the iron vehicle while another one flees in terror.[48]

The most famous experiment in America was the Tom Thumb steam engine designed and built by Peter Cooper in 1830 for the Baltimore and Ohio Railroad. It was about thirteen feet long and twelve feet high, and used local anthracite coal to fire a vertical boiler that produced steam to move pistons in vertically mounted cylinders that drove a wheel on one of the axles. This machine was challenged to a race with a horse-drawn carriage with passengers. The engine was able to pull ahead of the horse easily, but a belt slipped off the pulley and a valve broke, so the engine lost power, allowing the horse to win.[49]

On February 17, 1831, the Pennsylvania Legislature passed an act chartering a horse-drawn railroad company for the route between Philadelphia and Norristown.[50] Eight-thousand shares at fifty dollars each were quickly sold and even over-subscribed. The rails were laid ten miles from Philadelphia to Germantown, and the first car left the depot at Ninth and Green streets at 12:15 p.m. June 6, 1832. It arrived in Germantown forty-five minutes later, traveling at what was judged great speed. The fare was twenty-five cents, and cars left the depot every two hours for the trip when regular service was established.[51]

On November 23, 1832, however, Matthias William Baldwin of Philadelphia introduced a new technology. This was a steam-driven locomotive that could travel at twenty-eight miles per hour, an unheard-of speed at that time. It was successful. On the next day, November 24, Baldwin organized a demonstration, during which the locomotive pulled four cars with dignitaries from Philadelphia on a run to Germantown.[52] This was likely the trip that Gebhard took.

An engraving in a book by William Sloane Kennedy, *Wonders and Curiosities of the Railway*,[53] a boy's educational volume typical of the late nineteenth and early twentieth centuries, shows this "First Railroad Train in Pennsylvania."[54] It depicts a primitive engine supported by a pair of large driving wheels aft and a pair of smaller wheels in front. The railroad engine was named Old Ironsides, and was like the train Gebhard rode that day. The firebox for the long, horizontal boiler was vented with a tall smokestack. The affair was operated by one man standing at the rear of a platform in front of a rectangular car that held the fuel. Behind these were two coaches that looked like extended stagecoach cabs holding twenty passengers each on facing benches.[55] Around the flat roof of the coaches was a railing that would have held the passengers' luggage. A coachman sat on a high bench on the front of each cab with what appears to be the tall shaft of a brake lever near his left hand to control the vehicle. The cars were connected to one another by iron chains.

The engine weighed six tons. At the time, the directors of the company thought it was too heavy and almost rejected the project. The wheels were of "heavy cast-iron hubs, with wooden spokes and rims, and wrought-iron tires," attached to a wood frame that was outside the wheels. The driving wheels were fifty-four inches in diameter and the cylinders nine and one-half inches in diameter with a stroke of eighteen inches.[56] This locomotive was fired by locally produced coal.[57]

Old Ironsides had some mechanical difficulties that probably were much like those of the engine pulling the cars in which Gebhard rode. Sometimes, the "eccentrics" that transferred the motion of the lineal, reciprocating pistons into circular motion for the wheels would stick, preventing the train from moving in either direction.[58] There were other mechanical problems as well. Despite these difficulties, an advertisement announced daily runs, and a fare of twenty-five cents. In stormy weather, it assured passengers that a horse would be substituted for the steam engine.[59]

Gebhard's first excursion was about ten miles long, as Amy recalled. One of the mechanics who worked on this first run wrote:

> *At eight o'clock in the morning, she was first put in motion on the Germantown and Norristown Railroad at their depot, Ninth and Greene Streets. She ran a mile an hour, and was considered the wonder of the day.[60]*
>
> *The engine could pull thirty tons on a level track. It was found that the wheels were too light to draw the tender, however, so, to obviate this difficulty we had the tender placed in front of the engine, which kept the wheels on the track. Mr. Baldwin, the machinist, and myself pushed the engine ahead, until we obtained some speed, when we all jumped on the engine, our weight keeping the wheels from slipping on the track.[61]*

But, the small boiler could not build up a big enough head of steam, thus the locomotive could keep the train moving

Ernst F. Tonsing

only short distances. During much of the trip from Philadelphia to Germantown, the engineer and two of the crew alternately had to jump off and push, and then jump back on board. The crew and passengers rested at a hotel at the Germantown terminal and then got underway again.

The mechanic wrote:

> *At four o'clock we started on our return to Philadelphia, alternately riding and pushing in the same manner that we had come. Upon arriving at a turn on the road, at the up-grade, the engine suddenly stopped, when, upon examination, it was found that the connecting pipe between the water-tank and the boiler had been frozen, and the steam was all out of the boiler. It was then about eight o'clock, and was growing each moment colder.*

With the winter darkness and the temperature plummeting, the crew knew they had to take emergency measures.

> *"Necessity knows no law," and so, after a short consultation, we made a summary appropriation of sundry panels of a post-and-rail fence close to the track, and started a fire underneath the pipe to thaw it. In a short time thereafter we had steam up and resumed our journey toward Philadelphia, arriving at the depot about eleven o'clock.[62]*

This ride must have been quite an experience. As there was no spark-arrestor on the smokestack, the occupants were assailed by burning embers and choked by the thick smoke. Considering the narrow gauge of the tracks, the relatively small wheels of the cabs, and the very high seats for the passengers as depicted in the engraving, the affair looks rather unstable and must have swayed wildly back and forth making the passengers rather nauseated.

An amusing description of a journey on a wood-burning locomotive of the Mohawk & Hudson Railroad running a similar trip between Albany and Schenectady, New York, on August 9, 1831, gives a glimpse of what Amelia's great-grandfather's first railroad ride was like. The adventure began when the conductor climbed to his seat on the tender and blew a horn:

> *The engine gave a great jerk and the crowd burst into cheers. It was not a smooth start; quite the contrary in fact; the tender was fastened to the locomotive by a chain made of three large links, the chain was two to three feet slack, the first passenger carriage was attached in a similar manner to the tender and the second coach to the first and also the flat cars following the carriages. Therefore, when the engine started, it took up the slack by jerks and bounced the unwary passengers out of their seats. The locomotive jumped forward so quickly that the engineer only kept from being flung backward by seizing a support and hanging on to it.*[63]

After the passengers untangled themselves and regained their seats, the chimney gave a great belch of black smoke filling the cars with burning sparks. Pandemonium broke out as the victims began pounding one another to extinguish their burning clothes. Then, when the engine stopped to take on water for the boilers, another disquieting episode occurred:

*There, opposite the tank, the engineer pushed a lever
that was designed to apply brakes to the wheels and
slow the train. The contrivance worked admirably; the
engine was abruptly checked, the tender bumped into
the locomotive, the first passenger carriage crashed
against the tender, the second coach rammed the first,
and each of the flat cars catapulted into the one in
front of it. The passengers, still fighting sparks, were
again sent sprawling, now backward from their seats
instead of forward as they had been jerked when the
train started.*[64]

On the return, the engine ran out of fuel, so the engineer
tore up a picket fence conveniently located near the rails for
wood to burn. The passengers, too, saw an opportunity, and
disembarked quickly and tore up more of the farmer's fence
and wedged the posts between the cars so that the jerking
motion would not tumble the occupants. That saved the
day, and the rest of the journey was without incident. The
horses that were pulling buggies on roads near the tracks
were frightened by the train, however:

*[The horses] wheeled, upsetting buggies, carriages,
and wagons, and leaving for parts unknown to the
passengers, if not to their owners, and it is not now
positively known if some of them have yet stopped.*[65]

Nothing like this was recorded by Amy about Gebhard's
first ride, but probably the experiences on these other runs
were similar to Amelia's great-grandfather's jaunt.

Amy reports that her grandmother was terrified for
her husband when he left for this trip. Given the primitive

nature of railroad technology in 1832, it is no wonder that Maria Grace was alarmed. According to Amy, her grandmother "felt she would never see him again when he left the house to board the train." Gebhard, however, was elated by the trip, and when he returned, he declared that he "felt there was a future for such a mode of travel."[66]

Amy remarked:

What would he think of our trains today, especially those between Philadelphia and New York, and when Amelia and I have made the trip in 15 minutes by plane, with a favourable [sic] wind.[67]

Chapter Five

THE INTREPID GRANDFATHER DAVID EARHART

David Earhart

Amelia's family on her father's side was as remarkable and adventuresome as that of her mother's. Her
father, Edwin Stanton Earhart, was a great-grandson
of John Earhart (Johann Ehrhardt) who had immigrated

to York County, Pennsylvania, from Prussia in 1750. John served in the 10th Pennsylvania Regiment of the Lines in the Revolutionary War.[68] This unit was raised September 16, 1776, at Philadelphia, and was assigned to Gen. George Washington's main army. He fought in the fierce battle at Brandywine in which more forces were engaged than in any other battle in the Revolutionary War, and was the longest, continuous battle in the war, extending eleven hours. He also participated in the battles of Paoli, Germantown, Monmouth, Springfield, and Bull's Ferry, before his unit disbanded at the end of the war at Trenton, New Jersey, on January 17, 1781.

Edwin's father, the Rev. David Earhart, also was a courageous example for Amelia. He was born in York or Indiana County, Pennsylvania, on February 28, 1818, and on November 16, 1841, married Mary Wells Patton (September 28, 1821 or 1822-May 19, 1893). They had twelve children, of which Edwin, Amelia's father, was the sixth.[69] David was well-educated, having attended the academy in the city of Indiana, Pennsylvania, and studied theology at Wooster, Ohio. Ordained to the ministry in the Evangelical Lutheran General Synod, David served a series of parishes in southwest Pennsylvania. He was strongly against drinking alcohol and the institution of slavery, and he spoke about both of these evils relentlessly not only from the pulpit but also in his frequent lectures.[70]

David Earhart kept a journal from June 4, 1845, until December 31, 1875.[71] Many of the 110 pages are indistinct or smudged, but most of the important entries are quite legible. The early passages are written in a careful, elegant, but informal hand on unlined pages. The later pages retained these characteristics, but haste and the emotions of the circumstances are revealed in the uneven lines, varied heights of the letters, the uneven spacing of the words, and the many scratch-outs. The journal begins when David was twenty-seven years old and had married Mary three and one-half years earlier.

In this chronicle, David displayed the tremendous energy and tenacity that was to characterize his years in the Kansas Territory. He recorded visits to the sick, sometimes at some distance, holding Confirmation classes, preaching, conducting prayer meetings, weddings, Baptisms, Communions, funerals, and speeches delivered. Hardly a day passed without some pastoral activity in the towns and countryside around his home in Leechburg in southwest Pennsylvania. He was indefatigable in organizing churches. For example, on December 6 and 10, 1846, he led congregations in adopting a charter. On May 26, 1847, he laid the cornerstone of an Evangelical Lutheran Church at Pasavant Cook's Schoolhouse, and the following September 7, the cornerstone of a church in Prospect. He participated in another cornerstone laying September 27, 1849, the dedication of Mt. Pisgah Evangelical Lutheran Church, October 3, 1849, and another cornerstone laying July 4, 1850.

As was customary in the Lutheran churches at that time, David was "licensed" to preach and perform the sacraments of Baptism and Communion in a supervised internship before ordination, at which time he would be accepted fully into the ministerium of pastors. A joyous note was sounded on August 30, 1848, when he "met in conference in Leechburg & continued with conference till the night of 31 & was ordained to preach the gospel."

One of the persistent themes in the journal was that in addition to his lectures on biblical themes, he delivered talks on temperance and attended temperance union meetings.[72] In the two decades before this, temperance organizations had concluded that complete abstinence from alcohol was the only way to eliminate drunkenness and the social disruption it caused. This was a pretty "hard sell" to the largely German-American immigrant towns in which David Earhart spoke, however. He did not mention his success in these talks, but he continued to receive invitations to speak, indicating that there was no great resistance to his message. In addition to all this, David was able to publish two small books, *Holy Baptism* and *The Lord's Supper*, in which he related aspects of these sacraments in dialogue form. These were received with acclaim in the Evangelical Lutheran General Synod.[73]

On October 25-27, 1852, David recorded that he was "quite unwell from cold & over labour." He was "still sick & unable for service" on October 30, but on this date he wrote a sad note about his two-year-old daughter:

> *At ¼ after 12 O'clock A.M. our Dear Sarah Catharine breathed her last. Peace to her ashes & rest to her soul. Same day buried her but I was not able to go to the grave yard along with the funeral[.] this was the second death in our family & neither funeral was I able to attend in consequence of sickness.[74]*

David and Mary suffered other tragedies, yet there were some joys. He wrote on October 20, 1959:

> *We had another child born which is the 10th child & a son being the 5th son. God has blessed us with 10 children 5 sons & 5 daughters. 3 are not & 7 are living,*

yet May God give them grace to live to his honor &
glory & at last to die in the true faith of Christ & all
live again with Christ in Heaven above.

The tenth like all the rest I have consecrated to
God in prayer & intend to give it to God also in Holy
Baptism at the earliest opportunity. I regard it both a
privilege & a duty to give back to God in holy [Bap-
tism] the little ones he intrusts [sic] us with.

The newspapers and journals at the time were filled with events
in the Kansas Territory and the struggle there against slavery.
The passing of the Kansas-Nebraska Act in May of 1854 meant
that whether the territory was to have slavery in it or not, and
ultimately, whether Kansas would enter the Union as a slave
state or a free state, depended upon a popular vote. Afraid
that a free state might be created on its western border that
would attract their slaves to escape, the slaveholders in Missouri began to stream into the territory buying up the good
farmland, intending to bring their slaves there to work the soil.

Whenever there was a vote, pro-slavery non-residents
from Missouri and the South crowded into the voting sta-
tions, overwhelming anti-slavery voters. They were not
above using intimidation, fraud, and even guns to ensure
that the balloting went their way. These armed invaders
were known as Border Ruffians, and the resulting conflicts
gave the territory its nickname—Bleeding Kansas.

Alarmed at the situation, citizens of the North, many
sponsored by the New England Emigrant Aid Company,
began to move to Kansas in order to make it a territory
without slavery. They founded towns such as Lawrence,
Topeka, and Manhattan, just as the pro-slavery people had
founded Atchison, Leavenworth, and Lecompton.

The well-known abolitionist, John Brown, fought four hundred pro-slavery forces at the Battle of Osawatomie in August 1856, while at the same time, thousands of pro-slavery men, organized into armies, entered the territory elsewhere. A fragile peace, mediated by the territorial governor, John W. Geary, was broken repeatedly, one of the last times being the Marais des Cygnes Massacre in 1858, in which the Ruffians killed five anti-slavery men.

David opposed the expansion of slavery into the Kansas Territory and realized that if the southern states were able to establish human bondage in Kansas, there would be nothing to stop them from extending the institution into every United States territory. He took some time off in 1859 to go to the territory to explore whether he could move to Kansas. He was able to purchase some farmland near the town of Grasshopper Falls (today Valley Falls), and returned for his family.[75] Before he left, he was commissioned as a "special agent" of the Pittsburg Lutheran Synod and was authorized by it to purchase lots to build churches in promising towns. Then he, his family, and a group of his parishioners traveled in early 1860 by steamboat from Pennsylvania to Kansas and settled in Sumner, a small town three miles downstream from Atchison.[76]

These were dangerous times. The Free-Soilers—those who insisted that the territory remain free of slavery—were scattered and unorganized, while the groups from Missouri and the southern states were members of organized bands and militias. The Rev. Pardee Butler, a prominent Free-Stater, wrote chilling accounts of how the towns of Atchison, Doniphan, Sumner, Port William and Kickapoo were scenes of violence and "high handed outrage." Pardee, himself, was tarred and feathered, and placed on a flimsy, log raft at the levee in Atchison to float down the Missouri River for refusing to sign a loyalty oath to the Slavery Party. It was intended for him to drown in the swirling, swift waters, but he found a way to make it back to shore instead, where he returned home to continue his fight against slavery.[77]

David Earhart was just as energetic in the Kansas Territory as he had been in Pennsylvania. He organized a Lutheran church in Sumner while farming the land he had purchased. He also began working at churches at Pardee and Monrovia, and in May 1860, organized a church at Vineland in Douglas County, nine miles south of Lawrence. Then, in 1861, he organized other congregations at Brush Creek, north of Atchison in Doniphan County, and several more in that county as well as west of Doniphan County, in Brown County. He also began to hold services in St. Joseph, Missouri.[78]

David also was active in promoting education in the Kansas Territory and the state. He served as a regent of the State Agricultural College for six years. A special interest of his was the founding of Midland College in Atchison, Kansas.[79]

During the summer of 1861, a tornado rampaged through Sumner destroying most of the buildings, including the one in which David's congregation had been meeting. Most of the residents moved to Atchison, leaving the town almost vacant, and the church David had founded was closed. The Earhart family then followed their friends and neighbors to the larger city.[80]

From 1860 to 1868, David continued to minister to widely scattered congregations in the eastern and northern parts of the territory, which he did with considerable faithfulness and vigor. It required him to make the rounds of preaching points in Doniphan, Brown, Atchison, and Jefferson counties, and nearly through Douglas County to reach Vineland, a distance of some seventy miles, as well as making a side journey to Topeka or Stranger Creek. This was about 150 miles, and it took three weeks to complete the circuit, all at a time when there were no roads through the wilderness or bridges over the often-turbulent streams.

To attend to these congregations, he drove a two-wheeled, springless cart drawn by a tough pony.[81] Hamilton A. Ott, chronicler of the early days of the Lutheran church in Kansas, wrote:

> *Often did his friends remonstrate with him over taking such long drives when the weather was stormy, but the courageous missionary would reply, "When I get there it will be fine weather and the service will then go on."*[82]

The intrepid pastor bore not only bad weather but illness. Ott told that:

> *on one of his long weary itinerant trips over the pathless prairie and through deeply wooded valleys, with only here and there a settler along the way, he took seriously ill, and tethering his horse, lay down on the prairie and for a time was unconscious. Upon coming to himself he again hitched in his pony and strapping himself to his cart let him go home, where after a long ride, loving hands helped him out and cared for him as he passed through a hard attack of billious [sic] fever.*[83]

The historian noted David's "dogged perseverance where others had given up the fight, as well as his all absorbing earnestness and positive Lutheran character" in founding churches, preaching, and lecturing throughout the eastern regions of the territory.[84]

When the congregations organized into a synod, there was considerable controversy as to whether the new body would affirm the 450-year-old, Lutheran *Augustana Confession* unaltered, or whether it would adopt a confession with certain articles watered down to accommodate the Reformed churches. David opposed the whole of the delegates in arguing earnestly that the doctrines of the weakened document were in conflict with the historic Lutheran church from its foundation. The force of his arguments swayed the assembly, and the *Unaltered Augsburg Confession* was ratified.[85]

Ott quoted the first Lutheran missionary to arrive in the territory, the Rev. Josiah B. McAfee, that "Brother Earhart was not only a most excellent preacher but an indefatigable [sic] worker. His work was always well and systematically done and thoroughly organized," and that "he was second to none in faithful, efficient, self-sacrificing labors for the Master and His church, and when he shall cease from his labors his good works will follow him."[86] Recalling the legendary brave and wise Greek king of Pylos in Homer's *Odyssey*, Ott wrote of David Earhart that:

> *He should be styled the Nestor among our sturdy pioneers. None labored so long as he in this pioneer work, and none endured such trials, hardships, and privations, none sacrificed as freely in time and physical labor, and none left such permanent results of his labors as he.*[87]

When his wife died in 1893, David went to live with his daughter, Harriet Earhart Monroe, in Philadelphia, but in his final years he lived in Kansas City with another daughter, Mary Louisa Earhart Woodward. He died August 13, 1903, just six years after Amelia was born. It is unlikely that Amelia ever saw him, but no doubt she heard her father tell of his trailblazing father whose courage and tenacity was legendary in the annals of early Kansas.

Chapter Six

"MOTHER MONROE"
HARRIET EARHART MONROE

Harriet Earhart Monroe

S he was called "Mother Monroe," and was Amelia Earhart's aunt—Amelia's father's sister.[88] A world traveler, educator, lecturer, author—and a person with a huge heart—Harriet Earhart Monroe was one of the best-known women not only in Atchison but in the nation at the time, and surely was an influence on the young Amelia. Some biographers are puzzled why Amelia interrupted her visit to her sister in Toronto during World War I to become a compassionate nurse to wounded Commonwealth soldiers, why she became a devoted social worker and counselor to immigrant children in Boston's Dennison House, or why she walked out from a stage and stood on a piano in the auditorium of a high school so she could be closer to her young audience.

Amelia's biographers hardly mention her famous aunt or make any reference to her at all.[89] One biographer suggests that her grandfather, Judge Alfred Otis, tried to remove any "contamination" from the Earhart side of the family in his daughter, Amy, and his granddaughters, Amelia and Muriel, and "to make it look as if the Earhart heritage didn't exist." He also was quite disdainful of women who worked rather than were "literate, well-read, and genteel, and idle." "Only poor women worked," he said.[90]

Harriet was very literate, well-read, and genteel, but she definitely was not idle. It is certain that Amelia knew about her famous aunt, and would have heartily approved of her remarkable accomplishments. Amelia no doubt read of Harriet's comings and goings announced in the daily newspapers,[91] and she could not avoid knowing the presence in Atchison of the prominent educational institution founded by her aunt, which many of her friends and cousins attended.

The second of twelve children, Harriet was born in Indiana, Pennsylvania, on August 21, 1842, to Mary Wells Patton and David Earhart, and came with them to the Kansas Territory in 1860 when she was eighteen years old.[92] There she saw firsthand the violent conflicts between the pro-slavery and anti-slavery partisans. Harriet was nineteen years old and teaching when the Civil War broke out. Since an invasion of Kansas by Confederate forces was thought to be coming,[93] she went to Clinton, Iowa, to teach until peace returned to the nation. Harriet came back after the war, married Aaron L. Monroe, and bore two children. However, her daughter died in infancy, and shortly thereafter her husband also died.

Harriet now had to find a way to support herself and her son, Eugene,[94] so in 1870 she founded a private school, the Atchison Institute. She owned and supervised the buildings and education in the school "in all its details,"[95] as well as taught English literature and rhetoric. The school grew rapidly, and by 1885 it had 215 students. Soon it was acknowledged as "the best private school in the State." When her health failed that year, she retired having tutored some 2,621 students.[96]

The Atchison Institute, continued, however, when the school was selected by the Board of Education of the General Synod Lutheran Church in Philadelphia, Pennsylvania, to become Midland College. On the college's opening day—September 15, 1887—Harriet held a reception and delivered a brief address to the board and new faculty, which included her brother, history professor Edward Stanton Earhart, the future father of Amelia.[97]

After Harriet gave up her school, she moved to Washington, D.C., for several years, and then to Philadelphia to be near her sister, Della Earhart Mayers.[98] There she took up writing for several western journals and went on speaking tours. The scope of her talks was wide: "on religious, artistic, war, temperance, personal, economic, and historical topics."[99] Harriet was ambitious on the podium: "From May 1888, to May 1891, she lectured sixty nights in Philadelphia, sixty-nine nights in Pittsburgh, sixteen nights in Washington, and twenty-five nights in New York and Brooklyn."[100]

A handbill advertising her speeches listed:

Interesting Places, Official and Literary
People of Washington,
With Seventy Stereopticon Illustrations.

Life of Christ,
With the Forty-eight Leading
Pictures of the World
Illustrating His Life on Earth.

A New Lecture.
Review of the Civil War, with 100 pictures
Prepared specially for this lecture, of battles,
Generals and incidents.

It further stated that "She will be pleased to arrange with Lecture Bureaus, Teacher's Institutes, Churches, G.A.R. [Grand Army of the Republic] Organizations, etc."[101]

Harriet not only lectured, but also traveled to Europe many times, and then organized tours to the Continent. One of her handbills advertised a "Trip to Europe" of four months leaving New York in April and sailing for France, then touring Italy, Switzerland, Germany, taking a steamer down the Rhine River, then seeing England, Scotland, and Ireland. She stated that the American embassies would receive them in at least three of these countries and the group would have the opportunity to meet "many eminent Americans abroad" as well as artists in the towns they visited. Harriet also promised carriage rides in the principal cities, including one from Naples to Vesuvius and Pompeii. All this was for the price of $1,000,[102] including ocean travel, railroads, hotels, transfers, escorts, servants, and porters' fees. In addition, she would make the trip a "liberal education in Art, History, Literature, and Architecture" by giving lectures throughout the tour.[103]

Harriet also wrote books—lots of them. There was a novel, *Past Thirty*, about a husband who takes his five-year-old son and runs away. They have harrowing adventures on a wagon-train journey to California. In the meantime, the wife spites the Fugitive Slave Law and assists slaves to escape their bondage. At last, the man confesses his sins to his son on his deathbed and tells him how to find his mother. Son and mother are reunited in an ending that would have delighted nineteenth-century readers.[104]

In another novel, *Heroine of the Mining Camp*, Harriet tells the story of a young girl, Jennie, who wants to join her father in a mining camp out west in Colorado. The father says to his wife: "I do wish John and Jennie could exchange brains; I don't see that a girl needs such a strong mind, but a boy always does."[105] If Amelia had read this book, she would have bristled at these words, yet she would have been delighted that Jennie is as intelligent and strong-willed as anyone, and that, in the end, she prevailed while breaking the norms for women and families of the day.

In 1895, Harriet published a book, *Historical Lutheranism: In One Hundred Questions and Answers*, in which she asked questions such as: "Where and when did the Reformation of the Church begin?" "Who was Martin Luther?" and "What incident occurred in his early life worthy of mention?"[106] She also wrote *The Life of Gustavus Adolphus II, the Hero-General of the Reformation*, a biography of the Swedish king who was the champion of Protestant religion but who lost his life in battle in 1632.[107]

Harriet returned to live in Washington, D.C., and from her knowledge of the city, she wrote what became a very popular book, *Washington—Its Sights and Insights*, giving descriptions of important places, buildings, and people in the capital city, from the presidents to prominent senators and representatives.[108] From experience gained teaching psychology at the Atchison Institute and her work as president of the board of trustees of a rescue mission, Harriet published *Twice-Born Men in America, or, The Psychology of Conversion as Seen by a Christian Psychologist in Rescue Mission Work*.[109]

Another book, *The Art and Science of Conversation and Treatises on Other Subjects Pertaining to Teaching*,[110] consisted of her ideas on politeness, home and family, attention to personal appearance, imagination, language, and how to read books. She listed exercises for three-minute talks on "Life as a Race," "Life as a Game," "Elements of Success," "Self-control," "Care and Use of Property," and "Having a Good Time." She instructed women on manners with "How, What, & When to Read—History, Biography, Science," and for men, she quoted proverbs from Horace Mann:

"You are to be kind, boys, generous."

"If there is a poor boy with ragged clothes, don't talk about rags in his hearing."

"If you see a lame boy, assign him some part in the game that doesn't require running."

"If there is a hungry one, give him part of your lunch."

"If there is a dull one, help him in his lessons."

For all students, she offered much advice. Quoting a Chinese proverb, she wrote:

> "Be hard on yourself and the world will be easy on you."

> "Gather the bricks and straw of knowledge, that you may build later in life."

> "Be true to your highest, do not trifle on the way; there is no such thing as making up lost time."[111]

For teachers, Harriet had particularly strong words:

> The State has committed to you its greatest interest, the education of its future citizens. Children and youth are entrusted to your care, not alone to see that they have knowledge of certain branches of study, but they are given to you to make the best men and women you can of the material. The knowledge which they obtain is but a means to that end. May no soul in eternity look in your face and say, "You had a chance to make a man of me, and you failed."[112]

For everyone, she suggested many etiquette guidelines:

> "In eating apples, pickles, or other harsh foods, keep the lips shut, so as to prevent noise."

> "Under no circumstances pick your teeth at the table, but if you take a toothpick when offered, wait until you rise before even placing it in your mouth."

"Practice your best manners at every meal, so that when you are among strangers you will be sure of yourself."

"Get ready to stand in the presence of kings. To do this, you must not only have the knowledge and integrity of true nobility, but you must appropriate to yourself those delicate touches of exterior culture which distinguishes the higher classes."[113]

It is hard to know whether Amelia, a voracious reader, ever saw her aunt's books. Certainly, they would not have been on a bookshelf in her grandfather's house. Perhaps copies were available in the nearby home of her Tonsing cousins. Whether or not Amelia read them, she heeded their advice and displayed her character and manners as a guest of Eleanor and President Franklin Roosevelt during her frequent stays in the White House and in the royal palaces of England and Europe.

In addition to her many activities, Harriet wrote and produced plays. The sponsor, usually a church, would provide the venue, actors, and stagehands while Harriet supplied the scripts as well as the stage props and costumes. Tragedy struck one of these endeavors in 1908, however, when the drama, *The Scottish Reformation* was performed by members of St. John's Lutheran Church in Boyertown in southeastern Pennsylvania. Harriet and her sister Della rehearsed the actors and singers. It had been performed many times before. Some sixty people were involved, and 312 tickets had been sold for the first of several performances in the Rhoads Opera House. It was eagerly anticipated for its innovative slide projection technology and spectacular staging.

The first two acts of the play went well. During the second intermission, however, the young man operating the projector turned the wrong knob on the machine and it spurted out some gas. This frightened those sitting nearby, and they made a dash for the exit. When some actors heard the noise, they looked out from behind the curtains. One of them accidentally kicked over a kerosene lamp, and the flammable liquid then exploded and spread to the footlights that, in turn, burst into flame, starting the curtains on fire. At first, the audience sat patiently waiting for the staff to extinguish the fire, but suddenly they realized it could not be done, and raced to escape the flames. The windows of the upstairs theater were three-and-one-half-feet high and sealed with bars. The one door to the outside, too, was barred, and the only inside steps leading down and out of the building were immediately jammed with people.

There was no exact count of how many were killed, but with nearly 400 people in attendance or associated with the production, an estimated 170 people died—one-tenth of the town's population—and seventy-five were injured seriously. [114]While Harriet was not present in the opera house at the time, Della was, and died in the blaze.[115]

Having lost so many people, her dear sister, and nearly all her earthly possessions, Harriet was cast adrift in sorrow. Spring and summer passed as she mourned the tragedy, but then she received a letter in late August from a George W. Wheeler, president of the Gospel Mission in Washington. He wrote:

*Come down to the Gospel Mission, look it over and
see if you care to come in with us in the work of saving*

souls. Unless we secure a woman of large executive ability, our work can scarcely go forward.[116]

She went the first week of September 1908, and was appalled at what she found:

> *I never saw or dreamed of such conditions. The very walls were alive with vermin. In the story above the chapel were fifteen vile beds, and on the third story above us, we saw a floor covered with dirty, wrinkled newspapers. I said, "Where do the men sleep?" "On the beds you saw on the third floor and on these newspapers."[117]*

Harriet immediately took charge, and went out on the streets and hired "a force of cleaners, whitewash men, scrubbers, sweepers, etc.," and also called a friend, the wife of a Presbyterian minister, and two others, "who were not afraid of work," and asked them to bring "buckets, scrub brushes, rags, soap, etc.," while she got some chemicals to rid the rooms of the vermin. The crew burned the bedding, cleaned the rooms, and "went over the walls three times with lime and carbolic acid."[118]

Within five days, the mission had been transformed. However, they had spent $25 for the materials, a large sum in those days,[119] and there was no money in the treasury. So, Harriet went to the pastor of Luther Place Memorial Church, where she was a member, and persuaded him to allow her to speak to the Sunday School. She got the money, $27, in less than five minutes, so effectively did she plead for the mission at the church.[120]

By winter, the mission had fifty clean beds, for which the

men paid ten cents per night. If they did not have the money, she allowed them to sleep there without paying. When the beds were filled, up to 50 men slept on the floor "with only the boards under them and no covers." She spoke so often to her church's Sunday School classes that a four-year-old pupil once announced when she saw Harriet approaching, "There comes Mrs. Sheets and Pillowcases again."[121]

There was no heat in the building except on the ground floor. Harriet recalled a "young, fair-haired man from Virginia, evidently well-born and bred," who came in one night wet and with a bad cold. He started to climb the stairs to the dormitory when Harriet urged him to stay by the fire and sleep on a bench in the chapel. He refused and went up to the top floor anyway. He was dead by morning. "I had wept all the way home, for I feared just what happened," Harriet wrote. After another death caused by the bitterly cold winter, she approached Mrs. Richard Butler, a wealthy Washington woman, who toured the mission and went immediately to a hardware store and got a stove for the third floor and a fire drum for the fourth.[122] In the following years, Harriet obtained bathing and other facilities, and even new buildings to care for the homeless and destitute of Washington, D.C. By the fall of 1909 she had 85 beds available.[123]

One evening after the chapel service, a well-dressed young man remained sitting in the first pew. When Harriet went over to him, he said to her: "I am just out of Moundsville [Penitentiary]; no one has spoken a kind word to me, I have had nothing to eat today; I see no way but to steal again." He was just twenty-two years old. Harriet put her hand on his shoulder and said to him: "Son, we will take care of you and get you work." After taking him around for days, trying to find him a job, and seeing doors shut to him when the word "penitentiary" was mentioned, she realized that the mission had to establish shops where the men could be employed and break free of the brutal cycle of crime and imprisonment.

Harriet went to businesses with offers, and by the fall of 1914, she was able to open a laundry as well as shops for woodcutting, ropemaking, printing, and chair caning, where men could work "rather than eat the bread of charity."[124]Harriet also opened a dining room where people could get a meal for one cent.[125]

Harriet Earhart Monroe was described briefly in a biographical dictionary under an entry about her father, David Earhart, as "a lady of the highest culture and refinement." It noted that she was well-known for her articles in magazines and newspapers and that she was "one of the leading educators of the day."[126] The account praised her as one of the most influential women of the nineteenth century:

> *Few men, in so short a time, have succeeded in accomplishing more than Mrs. Monroe, and the energy and zeal with which she has carried forward the work, and the abundant success of her efforts, are sufficient attestations of her remarkable powers of mind.*[127]

Harriet acquired the name "Mother Monroe" at the Gospel Mission in Washington, D.C. In an article about her by Nelson A. Mason in the *Lutheran Herald*, he recalled that each fall someone from Johnstown, Pennsylvania, sent her a carload of coal to heat the mission, "freight prepaid." Year after year she wrote the donor a note of thanks, but she did not know who was sending this large gift. At last, she asked whether the person in Johnstown knew her. He wrote back:

Mrs. Monroe, fifty years ago, when you were presi-
dent of the Atchison school, one day there came to
your door a widow and her little son. You took them
in—fed and cared for them until the mother found
employment, and then bade them Godspeed. I was
that little boy.

The load of coal continued to come to the mission long after "Mother Monroe's" death in 1927 at the age of 84.[128]

As an adult, Amelia Earhart, too, was "literate, well-read, and genteel," and definitely not idle. She always gave careful attention to children and engaged in many acts of kindness to the end of her life. While it can be questioned how much influence Aunt Harriet had on Amelia as she was growing up, Amelia resembled her aunt with her empathy, compassion, and certainly her "big heart."

Chapter Seven

THE INFLUENTIAL GRANDFATHER ALFRED OTIS

Alfred G. Otis in 1865

Amelia's grandfather on her mother's side, Alfred Gideon Otis, was the descendant of a Puritan family that came from Hingham, England, to Hingham, Massachusetts, in 1631. In his family were the first trained doctors (from Harvard and Yale) in Colonial America.

Alfred was just two generations removed from his famous cousin, the fiery James Otis (1725-1783), whose Writs of Assistance (which included the watchwords: "Taxation without representation is tyranny") against the British was called by John Adams the "opening gun of the Revolution" in which America gained its independence.[129]

Alfred was born in Cortland County, New York, on December 13, 1828. As a young child, he already was determined and energetic. When his family moved to a farm in Barry County in the new state of Michigan, life was hard; Alfred had to work from dawn to dusk. He decided he should get a classical education, so every night after the chores were done, Alfred would sit at a table and study Latin, Greek, and classical literature by the light of a candle. With the money from his first teaching post, Alfred enrolled in the Kalamazoo branch of Michigan University as a sophomore in 1849 and graduated in 1852. He taught awhile in Mississippi, but studied law at the same time. Alfred entered Louisville Law School in Kentucky and graduated in 1854, teaching law in Louisville until October 1855.

Alfred was a highly intelligent and curious person. Above all, he loved adventure and wanted to see everything thoroughly. He had read of distant California and decided in the early 1850s to explore it bottom to top. He sailed around Cape Horn in South America and then to North America, then up the almost eight hundred miles of the California coast, stopping in various ports. But this was not enough for him, so Alfred got off the ship and traveled by horse, carriage, and stagecoach passing through San Francisco, Monterey, San Luis Obispo, Los Angeles, and San Juan Capistrano before boarding another ship in San Diego to return home.[130]

Exciting news appeared in the newspapers about the opportunities in the newly opened Kansas Territory, and Alfred decided to see whether he could make it there. He went to Atchison on October 23, 1855, and "set out his shingle" advertising his law practice. There was no courthouse in the new town, so he held his sessions in a storeroom. Often, Alfred would have to ride out to the offices of county justices and would be gone nine or ten days. According to him, often during the summer "he lariated his horse and slept in a blanket on the prairie."[131]

In February 1860, Amelia Harres of a distinguished family in Philadelphia, arrived in Atchison to visit her sister, Mary, wife of Dr. William L. Challiss. Alfred and Amelia met, and, as the family story goes, "when she returned in the fall she took A.G. Otis' heart with her." He followed her back to Philadelphia in April 1862, where they were married.

Otis was associated with the Atchison Town Company, which had incorporated in 1855 to promote the city. In 1861 he formed a partnership with George W. Glick, a lawyer his age who recently had arrived from Ohio. This partnership lasted until 1873. Glick later became governor of the state of Kansas. Most of their legal business was in the state and federal courts, as well as the U.S. Land Office.

Otis was a Democrat, which then was mostly the political party of the South where he had lived, so he was always held in some suspicion by the Abolitionists who were working to rid the country of slavery. But Otis, too, hated slavery, disapproved of the Confederacy, and was a strong Union man. When the Civil War began, the governor of the new state called for all able men in Kansas to join in the fight. Alfred enlisted, and throughout the war, served bravely in Col. John A. Martin's 8th Kansas Volunteers, an infantry division that fought in the major battles in the western theater. Otis was mustered out of the Union Army and reached his home in Atchison on April 14, 1865, the day President Lincoln was assassinated.[132]

After the Civil War, Amelia's grandfather became wealthy through his law practice and real estate investments and was president of the Atchison Savings Bank. Otis and Glick were employed by the Central Branch of the Union Pacific Railroad from 1865 until 1873. Alfred was the first attorney in Atchison for the Missouri Pacific Railroad, but resigned when he was elected judge of the Second Judicial District on January 8, 1877. He served until January 1881.

Alfred also was a regent of the University of Kansas in Lawrence for six years. For all his reticence to countenance women in roles other than domestic, the judge expressed a quite different view when he spoke at the dedication of the university's Snow Hall on November 16, 1887. In reference to plans for additional facilities "for the comfort and convenience of the lady students," he said, "The university had always recognized [women's] right to an equal share with their brothers to all the privileges of a state education, and was now considering plans by which they could more readily and widely avail themselves of its advantages."[133]

When his future commander, John A. Martin, purchased Lots 3, 4, and 5 of Block 1 on First Street on March 7, 1859, the deed was notarized by Alfred.[134] Alfred then purchased Lots 1 and 2, Block 10, on First Street on January 30, 1861, for $1,000.[135] First Street was renamed Terrace through the efforts of Atchison's then-mayor, John A. Martin, who thought "First Street" sounded too much like the rundown ones by that name in many Eastern cities.

On that site, now 223 N. Terrace St., Amelia and Alfred erected a beautiful Gothic-style home. It was "the largest and finest house in Atchison when it was built,"[136] and had a commanding view of the river and east into Missouri. The couple had eight children (two died in infancy). One of them, Amelia (known as "Amy"), was the mother of Amelia Earhart. Amelia and Alfred purchased the lots in front of their house that extended down the limestone bluffs to the river and created a park with seats, swings, and a lookout. It became very popular with the townspeople of Atchison since there were no other parks in the city at that time. Their house is now the Amelia Earhart Birthplace Museum, operated by the Ninety-Nines—an international organization of women pilots—and visited by thousands of people each year.

The house was rectangular with a kitchen extending from the back. Later a solarium with many windows was built on the southwest side next to the kitchen so Amelia Otis could sew with plenty of light. There was a servants' quarters on the west and a dining room on the northwest end of the house. The dining room had arched stained-glass windows that brought lively colors into the room in daylight, and which glowed attractively at twilight. The ceiling was decorated with an elaborate, quatrefoil design, plaster longe and chandelier. Seated at the table with the soft light of candles or gas jets, the elegance of the room lent a formality to meals taken there.

I am not sure what Amelia thought of all of this formality when she was living with her grandparents, but later in her career, when she was dined by royalty in Belgium and Great Britain and in the White House in Washington, D.C., she probably thought back to her meals with her grandparents and was grateful to them for teaching her which fork to use and how to place the napkin on her lap.

Alfred and his wife were noted for their graciousness toward visitors. The editor of the *Abilene Chronicle* of Abilene, Kansas, attended an editors convention in Atchison in June 1878 and was quite taken by the couple's hospitality:

We were met by several of the good people of Atchison, and all taken to pleasant places. Col. [John A.] Martin, President of the Association, kindly took us in his charge, and drove us to the most pleasant place in the city, the residence of Judge A G. Otis, and we will long have the kindliest feelings for his partiality in so providing for us. Judge Otis is a fine, scholarly gentleman, and should be the happiest man in the world. With such an agreeable and accomplished companion, and such beautiful, bright and well-disciplined children, he has a home the gods might envy. His residence is a fine one, and his grounds very beautiful, situated on high ground near the river. Judge Otis, and his estimable lady and pleasant children will long be gratefully and pleasantly remembered by us, for the many kind attentions shown us.[137]

Deeply pious, Alfred was the chief warden of Trinity Episcopal Church. It was founded in 1857 with Alfred and Amelia Otis being some of the founding members. The congregation first met in homes and rented halls. When the courthouse was built in 1860, the church services were held there. Every Saturday, Amelia and other women would sweep out the courtroom and prepare it for services the next day. Amelia and Alfred were major contributors when Trinity Episcopal Church on South Fifth Street was constructed of native limestone in 1866. It was a Gothic-revival building patterned after one in Stonington, Connecticut, and designed by architect James C. Sidney. It was one of the finest churches west of the Missouri River and was listed on the National Register of Historic Places in 1985.

John A. Martin expressed the highest respect for Alfred, and upon his retirement in January 1881 introduced the speech for his friend with the following words:

> *The respect and confidence in which Judge Otis is held, by the members of his profession, is testified to by the complimentary resolutions adopted by the Bar of this county yesterday, and by the legal fraternity of other counties in the District during the past few weeks. He has made an able, impartial Judge, and his thorough integrity has never been questioned.[138]*

Amy Earhart was sorry that her father did not live to see Amelia fly. Amy wrote in her letter to cousin Ruth Tonsing, "I feel sure Amelia would have had him in the air and enjoying it had he been here when she began to fly, but Mother might have waited longer to take to the air."[139]

Chapter Eight

THE COUSIN WHO GOT WOMEN THE VOTE IDA CHALLISS MARTIN

*Wedding photograph of Ida Challiss and
John A. Martin, June 1, 1871*

nother person who Amelia Earhart certainly knew in Atchison when she was growing up was her mother's cousin, Ida Challiss Martin, who lived in a house a couple of hundred feet to the north, across Santa Fe Street. Most likely she talked with Ida while sitting on the porch overlooking the Missouri River or perhaps in the large library of the house.

Ida was born on May 25, 1851, in Philadelphia. Her parents gave her the name "Ida" for the fairy who cared for the baby god Zeus on Mount Ida in northern Greece. It also meant "hard-working," and was appropriate since Ida had to take care of her five younger sisters and three younger brothers when they were small. Her mother, Mary Ann Harres, married a New Jersey doctor William L. Challiss. His family originally was from Sussex, England, and went back over a thousand years.

Perhaps Ida entertained the young Amelia with stories of her youth. A couple of tales that Ida loved to tell were these: Once when her father and mother had to attend a meeting, one of the servants was left to watch Ida and her brother, Harry. When she was not looking, Ida and Harry got into their mother's closet, put on her necklaces and bracelets, fine silk clothes, and lace shawls, and took her fancy fans and walked over "as stately as queens" to show a neighbor across the street. When they got to the middle of the street, however, a horse and buggy came and knocked them over, grinding the pearls and fancy fans into the mud. Another time, her mother had bought some new shoes but had not worn them yet. Harry and Ida thought that they would make fine boats. When their mother came home they were "swimming the shoes" in the bathtub. Perhaps Ida didn't want to give Amelia too many ideas, however, since Amelia could come up with enough on her own.

Ida's father, William, was curious about the Kansas Territory, so in 1856, long before Kansas became a state, he took a trip west to see the land for himself. He and his brother rode on the steamboat called the *Meteor*. When the large paddlewheel ship arrived in Atchison, he knew that he wanted to live there. William also was a businessman and could foresee that there would be a great many people coming there to travel west on the Santa Fe and Oregon Trails. He bought a ferry called the *Red Rover* that used a horse to pull it across the river.

The *Red Rover* did not carry very many people or animals, however, so William went back to Evansville, Indiana, in the fall of 1856, to have a steam ferry built for him that was bigger and could make the crossing faster. When he was sailing it back to Atchison in November, the Missouri River froze over and the boat was stranded. William paid a local man to watch over it while he and his crew—all friends from New Jersey—made it back to Atchison. When there was a thaw, he returned to find that the caretaker had taken off and a squatter was living aboard, claiming the boat as his own. William had to pay the squatter $25 to leave, and they sailed the boat up to Atchison.[140] He named it the *Ida* in honor of his eldest daughter. His new ferry was able to carry 150 head of cattle along with passengers, and soon was bringing thousands of wagons and pioneers across the river who were heading west to Colorado, Utah, California, Oregon, and Washington.[141]

William went to New Jersey in April 1857 to bring his family back with him. They traveled by train to St. Louis, Missouri, and then took a riverboat down the Mississippi River and then up the Missouri River to Atchison. Ida later recalled that when they arrived at Atchison and got off the boat, there were men sitting around playing cards and using very bad language. Her mother made the children put their hands over their ears and walk past them as fast as they could. Second Street had not been "cut through" the bluff, and her parents, with "Uncle George carrying my little sister and leading me by the hand," struggled up the steep, three-hundred-foot slope from the levee where the riverboat had deposited them.[142] They were housed for a time by John Bennett, the father of Imogene Bennett, wife of George T. Challiss.[143] However, the children immediately came down with the measles. "That was our introduction to Kansas," Ida said.[144]

It was still very dangerous to come to the Kansas Territory. Pro-slavery people from Missouri and the South were terrorizing the Abolitionist settlers. William and Mary were Abolitionists and so they had to be wary. The Bennett house was one of the first built in Atchison, and they had been married in 1855 in that house by a minister brought down from St. Joseph, Missouri. It was a rather extraordinary wedding, as Ida told it. The pro-slavery citizens of the town at that time were quite hostile to newcomers who they suspected of harboring anti-slavery sentiments.

Here's what Ida said:

As we know, Kansas was the first battleground of the Civil War. Many pro-slavery men were here trying to make it a slave state. When this wedding occurred, they, of course, were not invited and proceeded to try and blow up the whole thing. They placed a keg of powder under the house and applied the fuse, but being damp it failed to go off.[145]

Dr. Challiss soon found a log cabin west of town for his family, but Ida's mother had to cook outdoors. They set up an iron stove under some trees to make the meals. There were wild pigs roaming around, and sometimes they would rush in and try to get the dinner that was cooking in the pots. They would burn their noses, knock over the pots, and run away. Mary Ann was busy all day long. Besides preparing the meals, she had to spin thread, weave, and sew clothes, and for light at night, she had to dip strings into wax over and over to make candles. Ida's father had three men to help on the farm, and her mother had to cook for them too. Later he purchased two strong oxen to pull the plow. These two oxen also drew their wagon to take them into Atchison each Sunday for services at First Baptist Church.

Amy Earhart knew these stories, and perhaps young Amelia did too. I am sure Amelia was amused by the one Ida told about Grandfather Gebhard and Grandmother Maria Grace visiting them from Philadelphia, and grandfather became ill. Ida wanted to do something for him. She was still very young, but since her father was a medical doctor, she went to her grandfather and asked, "Grandpa, are you sick?" He said, "Yes." So Ida went to the kitchen table and wrapped some sugar in paper just as she had seen her father prepare some medicines, and went back to her grandfather's bed. "Grandpa, if you have a heady-ache and the stomy-ache, take these powders every three minutes till you feel better. Open your mouth and take one now." Apparently, her grandfather soon got over his illness, no doubt due to Ida's "medicine."

Once when Ida's mother and father had visited some friends west of Atchison and were returning, they spotted an old cabin in the woods by a creek. It was sunset, and her mother saw "the clear stream, the lofty trees, the hills with the sun setting behind," and fell in love with it, so they purchased it. Thereafter, when Atchison was hot and humid in the middle of the summer, Ida's family would travel fifty miles west to that cabin to stay.

The cabin was in very bad shape. The ceiling and roof were partially gone, the windows broken, and the plaster falling. After a lot of hard work, they fixed it up, brought in some furniture, and made it like home. When the family first stayed there in June 1875, grasshoppers were eating everything green in Atchison. They used some chalk to write on the side of the wagon that took them there, "Good-bye Grasshoppers," and "Woodlawn or Bust." There were no roads, so they would go over fields of prairie grass and down into the creek beds. They would have to clatter across the rocks and through the water to get to the other side. Once, the water was too deep and they got mired in the middle, and Ida's father had to scramble over the tongue of the wagon and the horses to get to the shore. Then her mother had to toss each child to her husband on the bank of the stream.

The first residents of the cabin were bedbugs. It was a long time before they were able to see them "put their feet behind their ears and march uptown," as Ida's mother put it. When it rained, water poured in and they would have to hold an umbrella up over them through the night.

Shortly thereafter, William founded the town of Wood-lawn near the cabin, laying out streets and building houses, a state-of-the-art steam mill, and a store. He also erected a Baptist church, and the bell that the Challiss family donated to it still rings in the services each week. A post office was opened in 1881. William anticipated that the town would grow as he expected the railroad was going to pass through it. The road was diverted south, however, and the town's population dwindled.

Back in Atchison, the family was very active in the Baptist church. While they never held dances, the youth would gather for "socials" in the church hall. These had various themes. To raise money for their projects, they would have an ice cream social where they would bake cakes and cookies for days, and make ice cream with fresh cream, eggs, sugar, and vanilla, with ice from the blocks that had been cut from the Missouri River during the winter and stored in an icehouse.

At one social, Ida stood at a table selling flowers. A very handsome man came in and walked around looking at all of the items for sale. When he saw her, he came over to her table, pulled out his wallet, and purchased all of her flowers. She was flabbergasted.

Ida already knew this man since he lived north of her house on Terrace Street and was an important person in town being the owner and editor of the city's newspaper and its former mayor. John Alexander Martin had arrived in 1857 from Brownsville, Pennsylvania, with his Abolitionist parents and family. Just eighteen years old, John had purchased the infamous *Squatter Sovereign,* one of the most vile and violent pro-slavery newspapers in all of the South, changing its name to *Freedom's Champion.*

To cover the Territorial Constitutional Convention for his newspaper, John went to Wyandotte, now a suburb of Kansas City, Kansas, where it was to be held. The delegates had had difficulties securing a secretary, but when John arrived, they knew that they had found the right person. Over his protests that he was only twenty years old, too young yet to vote, he was made secretary of the convention, and, according to his daughter, Ruth Martin Tonsing, penned the Preamble and five of the nine Articles of the Constitution that was accepted by the U.S. Congress. Kansas became a state, but this upset the balance of slave and free states and precipitated the Civil War. When the war broke out, John joined the U.S. Army and rose quickly up the ranks commanding the 8th Kansas Volunteer Infantry Regiment. After fighting in nearly every major battle in the West, from Nashville, Perryville, Chickamauga, Chattanooga, Missionary Ridge, and Atlanta, John retired from the Army at the age of twenty-four as a brigadier general.

William Challiss, Ida's father, was not too sure that his daughter and John should get married. John was allowed only to see her on Sundays at church, so he began walking with the family back to their home, but he was never allowed inside the house. One Sunday he was conversing with William about a book he wanted to read, when the doctor invited him inside to get the book. From then on, John was allowed inside their home to court Ida.

It was two years before they were allowed to get married, however. In preparation for the wedding, Ida and John built a large, fourteen-room, brick house that overlooked the Missouri River. On June 1, 1871, the day of their wedding, John carried his new wife over the threshold and into the house for the first time. The house included a large library built to contain his growing collection of books. Nearly the whole street now was a cluster of cousins with adults and children mingling daily.

John had gone to cover the organization of the Republican Party in 1854 when he was working for the *Pittsburgh Commercial Journal*. The party was opposed to the

Kansas-Nebraska Act, which would allow slavery to be expanded into the western territories. When John arrived in Kansas, he was active in founding the Republican Party in the territory. John was the postmaster of Atchison three times, and then mayor. He also was selected as a delegate to the Republican National Conventions and served on its national board and as its secretary for years. When the United States celebrated the centenary of the Declaration of Independence in Philadelphia on July 4, 1876, John was on the planning board and was one of its vice presidents. He had to travel to Washington, D.C., and California by train and often took one of his children along so they could see the country.

John successfully ran for governor of Kansas in 1884 and was inaugurated in January 1885, serving two terms. Since the capital city, Topeka, had no residence for the governor's family, Ida remained in Atchison with the seven children while her husband commuted weekly to Topeka by train. A bill was brought up in the Legislature to permit women to vote in city and school elections and for school bonds, but many men opposed it, including John. He declared that if the bill came to his desk, he would veto it.

Meanwhile, Ida had become acquainted with some of the national leaders of the women's suffrage movement including Harriet Myers and Helen M. Gougar. Helen came to Kansas from Indiana in 1884 to lobby for a Kansas suffrage bill, arguing that the Fourteenth Amendment to the national Constitution guaranteed this right. Ida took up the challenge to try to persuade her husband to sign the bill, saying that if one-half of the people of the country could not vote, the United States was not a real democracy.

The House of Representatives brought up the woman's suffrage bill in February 1887. It was strongly opposed. John's newspaper, *The Champion*, noted that:

The debate was one of the most remarkable ever known in Kansas. The members took their texts from the Holy Scriptures, and from the pictures on the ceiling, and from every department of nature and art, and all of history, sacred and profane.[146]

Despite these arguments, it passed ninety-two in favor, twenty-two opposed, with one member changing his vote from "nay" to "aye" after the roll was called. Even after it was passed by both the House and Senate, it was far from certain that Gov. Martin would sign it. His wife's uncle, Luther Challiss, who was dead set against the bill, groused:

The cartoon in the GLOBE of Saturday represents women of the future attending the City Council with their babies. I protest. When women become councilmen they will leave their children at home with their husbands.[147]

Others joined in with their fears that soon, women would want to serve in the military: "Now the women have a right to vote, we presume that 'colonels' and 'majors' will soon develop among them."[148] When the bill was laid on John's desk in the governor's office, contrary to all expectations, he signed it. Ida's logic had prevailed. Thereafter, wherever Helen Gougar spoke, she mentioned that Gov. Martin "would have vetoed the bill but for [Ida's] request to the contrary."

Great effort was needed, now, to rally women to register to vote. Churches provided space for the campaign. The *Atchison Daily Globe* announced a meeting: "Helen M. Gougar, the eloquent and persistent advocate of woman's suffrage, will deliver a free lecture in the Congregational Church this evening. The people generally are respectfully invited."[149] The next day the newspaper recorded the size of the gathering: "The woman's suffrage meeting at the Congregational church last evening drew an immense crowd of ladies, and chairs had to be carried into the church to seat them."[150] Other successful meetings were held, and the papers revealed that Mayor Kelsey "became alarmed over the importance of the woman vote, and has given notice that a woman clerk will be placed in the city clerk's office, to encourage registration."[151]

On March 19, the *Daily Globe* announced that 112 women had registered in Atchison, and added: "Among those who registered to-day was Mrs. Governor Martin."[152] It was significant that the spouse of the state's governor had come forward, and her example carried weight. Ida Martin's diary notes that she wrote a letter to Helen Gougar, and the *Leavenworth Times* printed it:

> *At your request I write to inform you that I am a regularly qualified voter, having registered this morning. I have done it from a sense of duty, and hope I shall have no reason to regret it. About fifteen have registered before me, this morning. I suppose, according to the Patriot, I have fallen from the ranks of ladies into those of the women, but I am satisfied to be classed as a true woman.*

Commenting, the editor wrote: "The *Times* is pleased to note the action and the strong words of the wife of the governor. The action of this womanly woman will make her many warm friends among the Kansas women."[153]

Ida Challiss Martin, Amelia's mother's cousin, was very proud of her role in getting Kansas women the vote, and participated in every election thereafter. In 1932, despite failing health, she insisted that her son-in-law, Paul G. Tonsing, take her to the polls in the City Hall to vote. That was her last public appearance; she died within two weeks.

Amy Earhart went across the street to Ida's home frequently, and there are photographs of Ida in the Otis house.[154] Amelia certainly would have known the grandmother of her playmates and cousin of her mother. Amelia would have known, too, that Ida was the widow of one of the most beloved governors of Kansas, but also that she was the woman who got the vote for the state's women, a hero Amelia could emulate.

Chapter Nine

THE STOIC
AMY EARHART

Amy (Amelia) Otis Earhart

melia Earhart's mother, Amy, is one of the role models Amelia most admired. Amelia ("Amy") Otis, married Edwin Stanton Earhart October 16, 1895.[155] He was the son of Mary and David Earhart, and the "adored younger brother" of Harriet Earhart Monroe. He was described as "a handsome man," [with] "bright golden hair and brilliant dark eyes," and was a student in his sister's Atchison Institute.[156] From 1892 to 1893 he was a faculty member teaching American History at Midland College in Atchison, a school that grew out of this institute in Atchison. At first all went well. Ed was employed by the Rock Island Railroad office in Kansas City, Missouri, and the couple lived in a fully furnished house that her parents had given them. Daughter Amelia was born to them in 1897, and daughter Muriel in 1899. They moved to Kansas City, Kansas, in 1900, however, to be near Ed's sister. Amy was from a prominent, well-to-do family and was raised in luxury, while Ed was the son of an itinerant, poor, Lutheran pastor who farmed and taught school, and difficulties soon arose in the marriage. Ed got bored with his work and began tinkering with inventions hoping to secure some money. In May 1903, when his idea for a signal flag holder that could be attached to a train seemed promising, he left for Washington, D.C., to secure a patent for it. However, when Ed arrived, he found that a similar idea had been patented two years earlier. He returned home even more broke. Ed raised some funds by selling the law books his father-in-law had given him, but when Judge Otis heard about that, Otis was even more convinced that Ed was irresponsible and a poor husband. Amy was constantly worrying about how to feed her family.

Ed secured a job with the railroad in Des Moines, Iowa, in the summer of 1907, and Amy went to live with him

while their daughters stayed in Atchison with their grandparents. Ed lost that job, perhaps because of his drinking,
and it was a year before he was able to get another one as
a clerk in the freight office of the Great Northern Railway
in St. Paul, Minnesota. Again, Amy moved to be with him.
Even though Ed tried to control his consumption of alcohol, his occasional violent temper disturbed Amy, and it
was increasingly difficult to stay with him. Ed heard of a
job in Springfield, Missouri, in the spring of 1914, and the
family moved once more only to discover that it was only
a temporary one and Ed again was out of work. With that,
Amy took children to stay with friends in Chicago, where
Amelia enrolled in Hyde Park High School.

It was certainly hard on the children. Amelia already
had attended six high schools, and finally graduated from
Hyde Park High School in 1916. One can imagine the
anguish of the young girls as they repeatedly were forced
to pack their belongings, say goodbye to their friends, and
start over again in unfamiliar surroundings. Perhaps this
enabled Amelia to cope with crises and to make friends
easily later in her life.

The relationship between Ed and Amy Earhart already
had been strained when their first child was stillborn. Amy's
parents had always disapproved of her marriage to Ed,
and they did not oppose their daughter's divorce in 1924.
Amelia was heartbroken over her parents' separation. Years
later she reconciled with her father and their relationship
became very close.

After Ed Earhart died in 1930, family members talked
about his alcoholism. It has been mentioned in many books
and television. After a TV feature on Amelia screened in the
1970s, Ida Tonsing Denton, my father's twin sister, called

me. She was very angry about the television program and exclaimed over the phone: "Ed was not an alcoholic! There is no evidence that he was! We all knew him!"

The context is important, however. Kansas passed a statewide prohibition on alcohol in 1881 that remained law until 1948, longer than the other U.S. states. The Nineteenth Amendment banning the sale of alcohol had been ratified in 1919, and was in effect until 1933. The cousins in the Challiss, Martin, and Tonsing families, were committed Prohibitionists, and John A. Martin, Amelia's great-uncle, had been elected governor of the state of Kansas on the Prohibition platform. For them, a person who had taken even one drink in their life was considered an alcoholic. Today we have a different understanding of alcoholism, and Muriel Earhart Morrissey's description of her father in her biography of her sister, Amelia, makes it clear that Ed Earhart was an alcoholic, but later was able to quit drinking and transform his life.[157]

Amelia's mother, Amy, was a remarkable woman in her own right. She was stoic, strong, and quite athletic. Little known is the fact that she was one of the first women to climb Pikes Peak in Colorado, an altitude of 14,115 feet. She was "dressed in a corset and high-heeled boots," as my grandmother, Ruth Tonsing, put it, but that is what most women wore at the time. Several of the young men on the excursion had to turn back because of altitude sickness while Amy Earhart made it to the top. Grandmother said Amy was rather disdainful of those men and their inability to keep up with her.

A reporter on the *Atchison Globe* who had known Amy Earhart from her youth described the young Amy as "prim," and "rather tall, dark, [and] slender."[158] The same person once said to Amelia:

*"I cannot imagine your mother as the mother of a girl
who steps into an airplane to fly around the world as
you did." Amelia replied, "My mother often accom-
panies me when I fly. She steps into my plane, makes
herself comfortable, opens whatever book she happens
to be interested in, and reads.*[159]

Amy was very close to her cousin, Grandmother Tonsing,
and they wrote to each other almost every week. Cousin
Kitty MacKinnon[160] remembers that boxes of her letters
were on shelves in her parents' house since her mother
kept them all. Sadly, this precious correspondence has
been lost.[161]

Amelia was not interested in flying at first. She saw her
first airplane at the Iowa State Fair in Des Moines at the age
of ten. Her father urged Amelia to go on a flight, but when
she saw the flimsy, wire and wood plane, she resisted and
insisted that she was much more interested in the merry-
go-round.

She graduated from Hyde Park High School in Chicago in 1916, and entered Ogontz Junior College in Rydal,
Pennsylvania.

While visiting her sister during Christmas vacation in
1917, she met wounded soldiers returning from World War
I, so she entered nursing school to work in the Voluntary
Aid Detachment at Spandina Military Hospital, where she
became acquainted with some pilots. When she and a friend
were watching an exhibition put on by a World War I ace,
the pilot spotted the two women and dived at them. Rather
than being afraid, Amelia was thrilled by the experience.

She caught pneumonia and maxillary sinusitis, however,
and was hospitalized from November to December 1918,

and then went to her sister's home in Northampton, Massachusetts, to recover. There Amelia spent her time reading, teaching herself how to play the banjo, and learning mechanics. She suffered from chronic sinusitis throughout her life.

Amelia anticipated enrolling in Smith College in 1919, but changed her mind and entered Columbia University to study medicine. A year later, when her parents had reconciled and moved to California, Amelia went to join them. On December 28, 1920, she and her father went to an airfield in Long Beach where the future air racer Frank Hawks gave Amelia a ride. She immediately knew she wanted to fly and took various jobs, including as a photographer, a truck driver, and a secretary at a telephone office, where Amelia saved $1,000 for flying lessons. Her first lesson was at Kinner Field near Long Beach on January 3, 1921, by Anita "Neta" Snook.

When her mother moved to North Hollywood, Amelia went to work at the Pacific Telephone Company on Magnolia Boulevard to support her flying lessons. At the time, the best aircraft in the world were being built at the Lockheed plant in Burbank. There, Amelia purchased her first airplane from Bert Kinner who had built it at the Grand Central Airport in Glendale. She worked at the Burbank Airport with Paul Mantz, honing her flying skills.[162]

My father, Ernest F. Tonsing,[163] served as a chaplain in the U.S. Army in the Battle of the Bulge in Europe with the famed 104th "Timberwolf" Artillery Division. When the war ended in Europe, my father's unit was transferred to California to prepare for the expected invasion of Japan. My parents and I lived in San Luis Obispo on the central California coast, and later Morro Bay. We drove down several times to visit Amy Earhart.[164]

Amy's house in California was not large. The front door opened directly into the living room, with the dining room and kitchen lying beyond. I remember going into the living room and sitting very quietly as the adults talked. But, there were lots of interesting things to look at since various objects that Amelia had brought back from her flights were scattered around the room.

Cousin Tiffy Challiss Cappel and her family also visited Amy frequently. She recalled seeing souvenirs sent by Amelia from her travels, including two shrunken human heads about the size of a baseball on the mantle above the fireplace.[165] Perhaps Amelia had purchased them when she flew to Mexico City in 1935 and gave them to her mother.

The shrunken heads weren't there when we visited, however. As a young boy, I would have been intensely fascinated by them and would have inspected them carefully, although I am not sure I would have touched them. Perhaps Amy removed them before we arrived in deference to my father, a Lutheran pastor, thinking they might be offensive to him. I certainly would have liked to see them, however.

Amy was always happy to see us and made us feel very welcomed. After some conversation, we would go to a restaurant for lunch. When Grandmother Tonsing visited us in Morro Bay in 1945, we drove down to see Amy. She and my grandmother got along quite well and chatted throughout the meal. Amy wore black every time we saw her and always had the same black hat. I was mesmerized by that hat since it had a big, black feather that curled tightly around it. I couldn't for the life of me figure out how it stayed curved and attached to the crown of the hat. I thought she was rather stern since she did not speak much to my brother or me, but my parents and grandmother assured me Amy was a very sweet and gracious lady.

The conversations at her home and around the table during meals ranged from current affairs, my dad's experiences in the war in Europe, what was happening with various family members, but rarely about her daughter, Amelia. Once, when Grandmother Tonsing was with us, however, I remember Amy saying she had always hoped Amelia could return but was resigned to the fact that she had gone down at sea.[166] We did not spend much time discussing this topic when we visited her, however, since it had been just a few years earlier that Amelia disappeared and we knew Amy was still grieving for her daughter.

The last time I saw Amy was in the 1950s when she was visiting Grandmother Tonsing in Atchison. She, her daughter Muriel Earhart Morrissey, and cousin Lucy Challiss went in to talk with my grandmother while I was doing something in the yard. I had read in the newspaper that someone was saying Amelia was a spy for the United States and was actually on a mission to identify Japanese military positions on the islands in the Pacific Ocean. When the four women came outside, I ran up to them and blurted, "Tell me! I want to know! Was Amelia a spy?" They stopped suddenly Muriel, who was a very sweet-natured person who I liked very much, turned to me and said sternly, "I was closer to Amelia and know her better than anyone else. She certainly was NOT a spy. That would have gone against everything she was trying to do. She wanted so strongly to prove that a woman could fly around the world that"—and her next words are seared into my memory—"she would not compromise that mission for anything!" Amy and Lucy nodded their heads in agreement. I believed them.

Shortly afterward I sat with Grandmother Tonsing and asked what the women had talked about during their visit. She said that, among other things, they spoke about Amelia's going down at sea. My grandmother said Amelia's mother thought for some years that her daughter would return, and kept her things ready for her. In the end, however, Amy believed that Amelia had simply drowned at sea. Muriel, Amelia's sister, wrote in 1982:

We like to have our mysteries solved; I wish I could satisfy all of us by producing an unimpeachable solution. That I cannot do, and, at this point, I believe no one can. In concurrence with many who sail the beautiful and fickle Pacific and who now fly over her waters, I agree with Cmdr. Thompson's theory that Amelia's plane was submerged within seconds after her last radio message and within a hundred miles of Howland Island. The Electra, shattered by the impact with the high seas, sank with her passengers trapped in the twisted cockpit. In a deep abyss of the ocean's floor, the wreck will lie, a hostage of the sea, until one of the world's nuclear submarines may someday resurrect it.[167]

Chapter Ten

AMELIA'S LAST FLIGHT

Amelia Earhart, International Forest of Friendship,
Atchison, Kansas
Photograph by Ernst F. Tonsing

Each day for many years, Grandmother Ruth Tons-ing dutifully recorded her activities in her *Five Years Diary*. Her entries began with noting the high and low temperature, before she moved on to write about the day's events. Typically she reported on her family, the house, letters written, neighbors and friends visited, garden vegetables canned, and trips down from her home to the commercial center of Atchison. On July 4, 1937, however, there was terrible news:

*Sunday, July 4. Amelia Earhart & Noonan Pilot lost
in Pac. Ocean on flight across world "just for fun."*

The daily entries in early July showed her rising alarm:

*Monday, July 5. Amelia & Noonan still being
looked for in south seas.*

Tuesday, July 6. Amelia Earhart & Noonan still lost.

Wednesday, July 7. No word from Amelia Earhart.

Friday, July 9. No news of Amelia Earhart.

Saturday, July 10. No word from Amelia.

Eleven days later, the following heartbreaking note appeared in her Five Years Diary: "*Wednesday, July 21. All hope abandoned for Amelia & Noonan.*"

Behind these words in her diary was considerable heartache. The famous and beloved cousin had been lost at sea, and "All hope abandoned." One can only imagine the grief expressed in the conversations between family members. Grandmother Tonsing also kept what she called a "memory book," a scrapbook with marbled covers and gray pages,[168] onto which she glued articles and pictures from newspapers about the family and other items of interest. In this, she followed her mother's example. Ida Challiss Martin filled many such books with clippings about the family and her husband's tenure as governor of Kansas.[169]

Ruth was especially careful to cut and paste articles about Amelia's achievements, her preparations for her globe-circling flight, and the frantic days following her disappearance. From these clippings, it is clear that for a while after Amelia's disappearance, her mother, and indeed the world, thought she might be found. *The Sunday Item-Tribune* from New Orleans blared in its July 4 headlines, "BELIEVE AMELIA SAFE ON ISLAND." Reports of frequent radio signals of "SOS, SOS," were heard from the plane's radio, KHAQQ, and it was believed she went down on a coral atoll in the Pacific.[170]

Forty-two planes from the Navy aircraft carrier *Lexington,* their pilots' faces "smeared with grease as protection against the blazing tropic sun," joined the search covering a 265,000-mile area, nearly as large as Texas.[171] The Navy planes sent to look for Amelia and navigator Fred Noonan were turned back by a surprise snow and sleet storm, perhaps the same storm Amelia might have encountered, according to the paper. The U.S. Coast Guard cutter, the *Itasca,* was employed in looking for the wreckage in the waters near Howland Island, just a few miles north of the equator. Other ships were enlisted in the search, all to no avail.[172]

On Saturday, July 17, "Navy airmen, plagued by heat and blinding rain squalls," ended their search for Amelia Earhart and Frederick J. Noonan.[173] Frantic, Amelia's husband, George Palmer (G.P.) Putnam, carried on the search for his wife and even consulted an "internationally noted Seattle psychic," Gene Dennis, a one-time neighbor of Amelia's in Atchison, to aid in the search. In a series of long-distance conversations, G.P. agreed to send her a pair of Amelia's stockings and a handkerchief of Fred's to aid in her psychic efforts. In return, Gene gave him good news: Amelia Earhart "is alive and safe on a South Seas island and will be rescued 'possibly this weekend.'"[174]

On July 24, G.P. had it announced by his friend, Sydney S. Bowman of the Pan-Pacific Press Bureau in San Francisco, that he was putting up a cash award of $2,000 for any information that would "definitely clear up the mystery" of Amelia's disappearance.[175] Nothing turned up, and Amelia's relatives gradually came to the conclusion that she had died at sea. Amelia's uncle, Theodore Otis, was interviewed in Atchison, and said, "I feel sure that both Amelia and her navigator met death at least a week ago." He thought "a plane like that cannot stay afloat long on an ocean, and if they had landed on a reef or island they probably would have been able to communicate with ocean liners by radio."[176]

By the time my parents and I visited Amy Earhart about eight years later, she did not believe her daughter would be found alive. In an interview with a reporter from the *Atchison Daily Globe* on March 23, 1944, Amy told a reporter that she "did not hope for her daughter's return, but did hope for some definite word of what did happen 'away out there in the Pacific.'"[177]

On July 31, the mayor of Atchison, Albert H. Lehman, made a proclamation:

To The Citizens of Atchison:

Whereas, Amelia Earhart was dear to the hearts of the people of this community, as well as to the American people in general; and

    Whereas, Amelia Earhart was not only renowned in aeronautics but was a wholesome American character and personality; and

    Whereas, Amelia Earhart has died the death of the brave, and her memory should endure,

> *I, Albert H. Lehman, mayor of the city of Atchison,
> Kansas, do proclaim that Monday, August 2, 1937, is
> set apart in this city as a day for civic mourning, and
> I urge the citizenry to attend the memorial services
> in Memorial hall that evening, at sunset. Let not the
> good people of the birthplace of Amelia Earhart forget
> her great courage and her usefulness to a science.[178]*

The final mention of Amelia in Ruth Tonsing's *Five Year Diary* is about this memorial service:

> *Monday, August 2. In evening [Paul] Jr took me to
> Amelia Earhart Memorial at Memorial Hall.[179] Burris
> Jenkins of KC speaker.[180] Walked home.*

At this service, the well-known Jenkins repeated his sermon of the previous Sunday at the Community Church, Kansas City, in which he read these words of Amelia's poem:

> *How can life grant the boon of living, compensate
> For the dull grey ugliness and pregnant hate,
> Unless we dare!*

"That," he said, "was Amelia's motto and idea. She was born to dare, and when she failed she tried again. If she is indeed dead, she died as she would have liked to die."[181]

Amelia's destination, Howland Island, was low in the water, less than one mile in width, two in length, and would have been at the end of a long, exhausting flight. Coming from Lae, New Guinea, Howland would have had to be sighted after twenty hours of continuous flight. With no autopilot mechanism, Amelia would have been required to maintain intense concentration throughout the flight. With lack of oxygen, the noise of engines, gas fumes, and now it turns out, snow and sleet in an unusual weather event, it would have been an extraordinarily difficult flight. In addition, very little was known about jet lag at the time. The exertions leading up to this last flight would have contributed to Amelia's physical and mental exhaustion. It seems as if everything was against her during this next-to-last leg of her intended circumnavigation of the world.

Grief over Cousin Amelia's disappearance never lifted from the family in the ensuing years. Expressions of it often arose in their gatherings, particularly in July 1997, when some fifty relatives gathered in Atchison to commemorate what would have been Amelia's hundredth birthday. The bright, cheery, energetic, and engaging cousin many of them still remembered was gone and could no longer enervate their conversations and activities. Those present in Atchison that July, who had talked and played with Amelia in their youth, remained profoundly grief-stricken.

Chapter Eleven

AMELIA'S FAMILY REMEMBERS

Amelia's Family at the centennial of her birth, July 24, 1997

F ew people are left who remember meeting Amelia Earhart as children. One man with whom I spoke recalled her flying and landing in a small airport in Santa Paula, California, north of Los Angeles, in an "auto-gyro," the predecessor of the helicopter. He was about five or six years old at the time when she came over and talked with the little boy. I asked him what he thought of her, and he said that he thought she was a "very nice lady," and he was impressed that she would take the time to stop and chat with

Ernst F. Tonsing

a young boy when there were so many other people there.

One who knew Amelia as well as anyone, Mary Brashay, the housekeeper for the Otis family for over thirty years, said about Amelia's character in an interview with a reporter from the *Atchison Daily Globe*, that "Millie was always the most lovable girl imaginable." She was like that throughout her adult life.[182]

Amelia began planning early in 1936 to make a daring flight around the world. On March 17, 1937, her preparations complete, she took off going west from Oakland, California, and landed on Luke Field, Honolulu. With co-pilot Paul Mantz, navigator Fred Noonan, and her plane loaded with fuel, she took off early the morning of March 20 for the second leg of her flight. Fred was to navigate to Howland Island in the Pacific, and Paul would continue to Australia, the most hazardous parts of the flight. Amelia then would continue solo around the rest of the world returning to Oakland.

During the takeoff, however, a wheel hit a pothole and the right landing gear broke off, spinning her around. The crew was unhurt but badly shaken. Diane Seal of Thousand Oaks, California, told me her father was one of the crew who worked on Amelia's plane after it crashed. Diane gave me a framed clipping from the *Honolulu Advertiser* that her father had saved. It has six photographs of the damaged plane and the dazed pilot. The captions describe sailors and personnel at Luke Field examining the landing gear, which was "snapped off after a blowout during the takeoff," and which "lay 25 yards from the crumpled Lockheed."

Along with the newspaper clipping, Diane shared several photographs that had been her father's. One showed Paul, Amelia, and Fred as they were being interviewed following the crash. After being unnerved by the disaster, it is remarkable that Amelia managed to give a smile to the photographer despite her disappointment at interrupting her round-the-world flight. Her indomitable spirit and gracious manners sustained her even then.

In addition, "she was always quite feminine," according to Marian "Mim" Overholser, another woman with whom I spoke. Mim was much younger than Amelia, but she befriended her, and they often went flying together. She said Amelia always had a lot of energy, and even though the days were exhausting, she always loved to go out dancing at night.[183]

The recollections of Amelia's family reveal many sides of her personality. My father's twin sister, Aunt Ida Tonsing Denton, told about the wonderful times her siblings had with Amelia—the piles of toys in the Tonsing house to be played with hidden under the staircase in the hallway. Grandmother Tonsing talked about the Otis family's horse barn across Terrace Street on the Missouri River side that was the site of innumerable games for the children. Grandmother insisted Amelia was not what one would call a "tomboy." Today I think that we would describe Amelia as being "outgoing" and "sporty."

Kitty Mellenbruch MacKinnon of Salem, Oregon, daughter of Orpah Tonsing who played with Amelia when they were young, recalled that she was about six years old (that is, about 1936), when Amelia flew into Springfield, Ohio. Kitty was home from school that day, and she and her mother went out to the airport. She was impressed by the large crowds there and by the big plane that landed. Kitty said she was even more amazed when a <u>woman</u> climbed out of the plane and came right over to her mother and hugged her. She thought Amelia must have hugged her, too, but she didn't remember. She was just too absorbed in staring at the huge crowd.[184]

Another of Amelia's cousins, Ralph Martin, from Brenham, Texas, mentioned he was about nine years old when his father took him to meet Amelia when she was visiting Atchison in the summer of 1935. He didn't have much of a conversation with her other than telling her the family members "were all proud of the things she had done."

Another recollection of Amelia is from cousin Tiffy Challiss Cappel, of Sun Valley, Idaho, who related:

> *My father, Jack Challiss [son of Dr. William and Mary Challiss], often was put in charge of the younger girls, often including cousins Amelia and Muriel Earhart. The group of kids would go into the barn, and in order to keep the younger ones occupied, Jack would use his great imagination to create a game with rules that changed at every play. It would start something like "Cops and Robbers," shift to "Cowboys and Indians," and then to something else again, keyed to the narrative, which Jack told as the game unfolded. Amelia was especially excited when they were to do the game, and insisted on continuing to play even though the other children had lost their interest in it.[185]*

Amelia loved to be with Jack Challiss since he told the most hilarious events with all seriousness, even though everyone was laughing hysterically. Tiffy described a surprise visit Amelia paid him at their home in Los Angeles:

> *Amelia was in the Los Angeles area and visited Jack*

one day. No one was home, so she made herself at home by going into the kitchen and searching for something to eat in the kitchen. My mother came home and walked into her kitchen to see the back end of some stranger—she had never met Amelia—sticking out of the refrigerator and demanded to know who this was, and was surprised to find that this was Amelia Earhart. My mother was a very proper lady, and she never quite got over the event, thinking that it was unseemly for Amelia to have been so familiar in a home that was not hers![186]

Chapter Twelve

AMELIA'S MOST
IMPORTANT FLIGHT

Statue of Amelia Earhart by Ernst Shelton,
North Hollywood, California
Photograph by Ernst F. Tonsing

Cousin Amelia

T oo much attention is given to Amelia's disappearance; it is her life that is important and the inspiration she has provided to generations of women and men. Recently, I spoke to a grade school in The Woodlands, Texas, and two-hundred-fifty students lined up to shake my hand. They had all read about her in their classes and were thrilled to hear more about her from a member of her family. In Topeka, Kansas, ninety-six-year-old Louise Corrick told me she had followed every part of Amelia's life and that Amelia was one of her greatest inspirations. At the small airport in Santa Paula in southern California, a white-haired man over ninety years old came up to me and related how, as a child, he was present when Amelia flew in and landed in a gyrocopter and how she spoke so kindly to him. It inspired him to become a pilot too. One hears similar stories from men as well as women everywhere.

Amelia Earhart was a heroic woman. The subject of more than one hundred books and thousands of articles, she has museums, libraries, airports, and even a ship named after her. She was an engaging lecturer as well as a competent automobile mechanic. She danced with the Prince of Wales, the future King of England, and loved tuna fish sandwiches and tomato juice. She was a compassionate nurse to injured and maimed soldiers during World War I and an enthusiastic teacher at the Denison House in Boston, introducing new immigrants to the mysteries of the English language.

Amelia was a contributing editor of journals and magazines, wrote books,[187] and even designed "active living" clothes and lightweight luggage.[188] Certainly, she was a pioneer in aviation, taking the controls of an airplane when most women did not even drive automobiles. She, as well as other noteworthy women of her day, refused to accept the idea that women should not fly airplanes.

Amelia flew at a time when opportunities for women pilots were quite limited, however, and they were relegated to second class. They had to fly smaller and less-expensive planes than men and had fewer opportunities to get air time (the men had the advantage of training in the armed services). It is startling to know that it was only in the late 1950s that United Airlines dropped the ban on female passengers on the New York to Chicago "executive flights." Amelia thought strongly that separate records should be kept for women to highlight their achievements.[189]

Amelia gave hundreds of lectures to promote opportunities for women not only in aviation but in other fields as well. She looked to the day that both men and women were valued for their abilities:

> It has always seemed to me that boys and girls are educated very differently...too often little attention is paid to individual talent. Instead, education goes on dividing people according to their sex, and putting them in little feminine or masculine pigeonholes.[190]

Amelia always had great optimism for the prospects of women. While she achieved much, many of her predictions for aviation and women were not accomplished during her lifetime. She and other women of her day set in place the foundations upon which later generations of women have built, however. The most important part of Amelia's life was her *life* and the inspiration it has given to others.

The following is from the talk that I delivered to Amelia Earhart's family in Atchison, Kansas, on the occasion of the hundredth anniversary of her birth, July 24, 1997.

The most important flight of Amelia Earhart was not her last flight, but her first. I have been wondering when it was that Amelia Earhart originally dreamed of flying. Perhaps it was some cold morning, looking out of her window at her grandparents' home in Atchison, across the road and through the leafless fall forest that she saw a bird rise from a tree limb and glide and turn out across the ol' Missouri River.

Or maybe it was when she was still younger, exploring the Kansas grasses that grew along the bluffs of the river that she spied even more wonders, for there are many things that fly besides birds— creepy grasshoppers, barrel-backed beetles, and also glossier cottonwood seeds. Even spiders spin out long, thin threads to the wind and then ride them to places dimly imagined in the tiny brains behind their multiple eyes.

Amelia was older when she read that humans had tried to fly—Leonardo da Vinci once invented a canvas corkscrew, which, however frantically hand-turned, moved nowhere. Maybe she read of the French who built balloons in the late eighteenth century and comical contraptions with wings in the nineteenth. And she would have read in the newspapers about Orville and Wilbur Wright at Kittyhawk, North Carolina, who made wings, which now enabled humans to surpass even the birds.

Even more, I have been wondering when Amelia first wove these cottonwood seeds and spiderwebs into ideas that could take wing in reality. The beginning of flight, one must understand, isn't the physical lift, the climb, the suspension over the abyss of atmosphere and earth; it is in dreams; it's when one envisions continents stitched together just as one sews patches together into quilts; it's when one draws a finger around a schoolroom globe making an imaginary line from one's hometown to the ocean, and then beyond from ocean to other oceans. Amelia Earhart made her first flight not with metal wings and a noisy propeller. She made it in her dreams.

But, if dreams, then what kind of fantasies were those that produced such daring physical feats and flights? Dreams as we know them cannot devise such things as Amelia did. Dreams appear in the night. They fly out of the unconscious, colliding with one another, multiplying in fantastic flowers of fantasy, evaporating and reappearing in psychedelic colors and forms. Birds and beetles and corkscrew contraptions in these dreams become only horrible monsters.

It wasn't night dreams that inspired Amelia Earhart to fly. It was not out of this dark delirium of shadows and veiled forms that flit about in the deepest recesses of the mind. It was the imagination, the daydreams that swirl before the eyes in spare moments of waking hours.

Do not be too swift to dismiss daydreams, for these are the ones we can shape, control, and direct. These we can mold and try in varying combinations and forms and arrangements. Night dreams need the arcane sorcery of mystics or psychiatrists to interpret. They are rarely predictive, prescriptive, or even useful. Daydreams, however, we can guide and glide. We can turn them about in the sky and send them off into new directions.

It is the imagination that lifts daydream wings into the air, and daydream flights from one Kansas town to other towns, from this continent to other continents, and from this earth to celestial bodies that exist in the imagination long before scientists locate their faint traces in slowly exposed emulsions behind their telescopes.

Amelia's family, and indeed, the world, celebrate her not as a dreamer, but as a daydreamer, not as one who fastened upon the fleeting forms of the night, but as one who spun forth ideas in the day, one who shaped those daydreams in her hands and then lifted them up into the air, into the realities of flight plans, instruments, propellers, and wings. It was her daydreams that started upon the bluffs of the Missouri River in Kansas and took her to heights and distances beyond which other humans then scarcely dared to imagine.

We celebrate Amelia Earhart, but our celebration is empty if we only commemorate. Celebration must also embrace a pledge—an oath that her daydreams will also unfold into dreams in our day, and that these dreams will, in turn, fly into dreams and realities in future days. Let the example of the imagination, courage, and heroism of Amelia Earhart enable us to dream. And mounting up upon the wings of our imaginations, let us dream even greater dreams, greater accomplishments, and greater flights of the human spirit.

APPENDIX: AMELIA EARHART'S FAMILY

as mentioned in this book[191]

HARRES-OTIS

Gebhard Harres (1801-1863)	Maria Grace Neville Harres (1797-1896)

Alfred Gideon Otis (1827-1912)	Amelia Josephine Harres (1837-1912)

Edwin Stanton Earhart (1867-1929)	Amelia [Amy] Otis Earhart (1867-1962)

Amelia Mary Earhart Putnam (1897-1937)	Muriel Grace Earhart Morrissey (1899-1998)

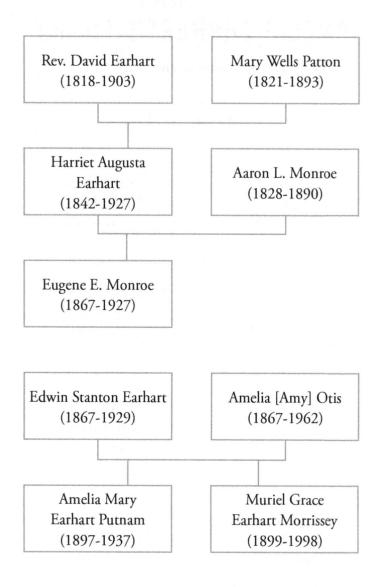

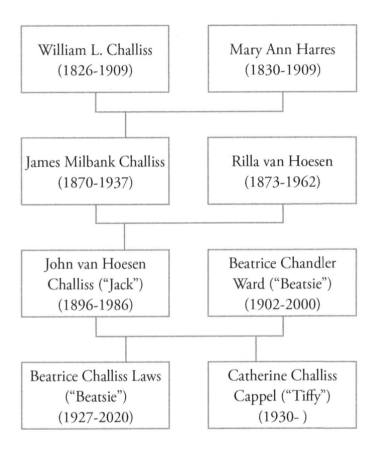

William L. Challiss (1826-1909)	Mary Ann Harres (1830-1909)
James Milbank Challiss (1870-1937)	Rilla van Hoesen (1873-1962)
John van Hoesen Challiss ("Jack") (1896-1986)	Beatrice Chandler Ward ("Beatsie") (1902-2000)
Beatrice Challiss Laws ("Beatsie") (1927-2020)	Catherine Challiss Cappel ("Tiffy") (1930-)

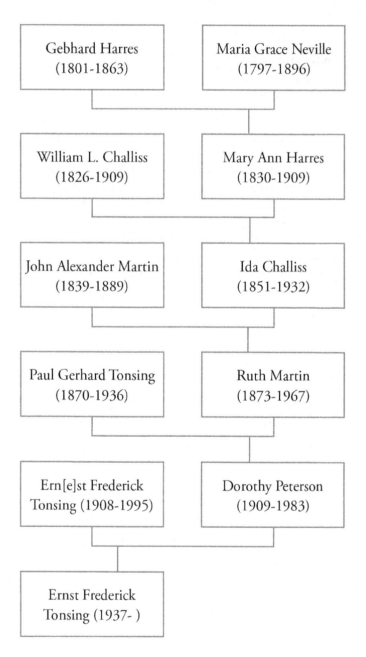

Gebhard Harres
(1801-1863)

Maria Grace Neville
(1797-1896)

William L. Challiss
(1826-1909)

Mary Ann Harres
(1830-1909)

John Alexander Martin
(1839-1889)

Ida Challiss
(1851-1932)

Paul Gerhard Tonsing
(1870-1936)

Ruth Martin
(1873-1967)

Ern[e]st Frederick
Tonsing (1908-1995)

Dorothy Peterson
(1909-1983)

Ernst Frederick
Tonsing (1937-)

ENDNOTES

1   **Among Amelia Earhart's notable achievements:** Received her flying license at age twenty-four, the sixteenth woman to do so (1921). Broke the women's altitude record of 14,000 feet (October 22, 1922). Held the women's speed record (June 25, 1930). Held the speed record of 181.18 mph (July 5, 1930). Held the women's autogyro (forerunner of the helicopter) altitude record of 18,415 feet (April 8, 1931).

First woman to cross the Atlantic Ocean by air (June 17-18, 1928). First woman to fly solo across the Atlantic Ocean (May 20-21, 1932). First woman to fly nonstop across the United States (August 24-25, 1932). First woman to fly in an autogyro (1931). First woman to fly across the United States in an autogyro (1931). First woman to hold the woman's non-stop transcontinental speed records flying 2,447.8 miles in 19 hours, 5 minutes (August 24-25, 1931). Broke her own speed record flying across the United States in 17 hours, 7 minutes (July 7-8, 1933). First woman to fly from Honolulu, Hawaii, to Oakland, California (January 11-12, 1935). First person to fly solo from Los Angeles to Mexico City (1935). First person to fly solo from Mexico City to New York (1935).

Began her flight around the world and was the first person to fly from the Red Sea to India (June 1, 1937).

Awards received: Special Gold Medal of the National Geographic Society, presented by President Herbert

Hoover (June 21, 1932). First woman to receive the Distinguished Flying Cross from Congress (July 29, 1932). Gimbel Award as the "Most Outstanding Woman of America" (1932). Decorated with a medal from the Kingdom of Romania (1930). First woman to enter the Aviation Hall of Fame, Dayton, Ohio (December 17, 1968).

Other accolades: In addition, Amelia has been honored with statues in the International Forest of Friendship, Atchison, Kansas; Topeka, Kansas, State Capitol; Perdue University campus, West Lafayette, Indiana; and others in Oakland, California, and North Hollywood, California. The Kansas Legislature approved a likeness of her in Statuary Hall in the U.S. Capitol. The airport and stadium in Atchison were named after her, and Highway 75 between Leavenworth and Horton, Kansas, was named the Amelia Earhart Memorial Highway in July 1987. The bridge across the Missouri River from Buchanan County, Missouri, to Atchison on Route 59 was named the Amelia Earhart Bridge in 1997 to honor the centennial of her birth. A giant earthwork portrait of Amelia visible from the air, composed of various stones and plantings, was constructed on a hillside by Kansas artist Stan Herd above Warnock Lake, southwest of Atchison in 1997. In North Hollywood, California, there is the Amelia M. Earhart Regional Branch, Los Angeles Public Library. There are many more such monuments to her found around the world.

2 *Research and Activities of State Geological Survey of Kansas* (Lawrence, Kansas: Kansas State Geological Survey, 1959), 28.

3   Due to inflation, $1,000 would be about equal to $30,942.62 in 2021.

4   J.H. Stringfellow, "Sketch of Atchison City, Kansas," in James Sutherland and Henry N. McEvoy, *Sutherland & McEvoy's Atchison Directory* (Clerk's Office of the District Court of the Territory of Kansas, 1859), 17-8.

5   "To Kansas Emigrants: The Atchison Steam Ferry," *Freedom's Champion* (April 3, 1858).

6   Frank A. Root and William Elsey Connelley, *The Overland Stage to California. Personal Reminiscences and Authentic History of the Great Overland Stage Line and Pony Express from the Missouri River to the Pacific Ocean* (Topeka: Published by the Authors, 1901), 409-10.

7   J. Gabside, "Ten Years Ago!" *Champion* (January 1, 1874).

8   Margaret Whittemore, *Historic Kansas: A Centenary Sketchbook* (Manhattan, Kansas: Flint Hills Book Company, 1954), 212.

9   "Overland Stage Line," *Freedom's Champion* (May 31, 1863).

10   John A. Martin, "The Champion," *Champion* (February 20, 1878).

11   Martin, "Atchison City, Kansas," *Champion* (April 3, 1858).

12   Martin, "Atchison Historically," *Champion* (January 2, 1881). The Atchison & St. Joseph Railroad later

became the Kansas City, St. Joseph & Council Bluffs Railroad.

13 The popular, Oscar-winning song, *On the Atchison, Topeka and the Santa Fe,* was written for a film in 1946 about the "Harvey Girls," the women who worked in the chain of Harvey House Restaurants along the tracks of the AT&SF Railroad. Sung by Judy Garland in the film, the song, with lyrics by Johnny Mercer and music by Harry Warren, was later sung by Bing Crosby, The Four Freshmen, Henry Mancini, John Denver, Rosemary Clooney, and others.

14 Root and Connelley, *The Overland Stage to California,* 419.

15 Mary Ann Harres was born May 29, 1830, in Philadelphia, and died April 30, 1909, in Toledo, Ohio. On August 1, 1850, she married William L. Challiss, who was born November 27, 1826, and died April 23, 1909. Rebecca Chaky and Ruth Martin, *Ruth Martin Family Tree 1995* (Friendsworth, Texas: Never Done Press, 1995), 28.

16 Ida Challiss was born May 25, 1851, in Moorestown, New Jersey, and died November 2, 1932, in Atchison, Kansas. On June 1, 1871, she married Col. John Alexander Martin, born May 10, 1839, in Brownsville, Pennsylvania, and died October 2, 1889, in Atchison, Kansas. Ibid., 51.

17 Ruth Martin was born May 30, 1873, in Atchison, Kansas, and died March 20, 1967, in Atchison. On September 7, 1893, she married Paul Gerhardt Tons-

ing, born January 3, 1870, in Cleveland, Ohio, and died March 1, 1936, in Atchison. Ibid., 92.

18   The maternal grandparents of Amelia Earhart, Amelia Josephine Harres was born February 1, 1837, in Philadelphia, and died February 2, 1912, in Atchison. On April 22, 1862, she married Alfred Gideon Otis, who was born December 13, 1827, in Cortland, New York, and died May 12, 1912, in Atchison. Ibid., 15.

19   Mary Wells Patton was born September 28, 1821(2), and died May 19, 1893. She married David Earhart November 16, 1841, who was born February 28, 1818, in York County, Pennsylvania, and died August 13, 1903. Ibid., 133.

20   This Gothic style, limestone church had been built in 1866, shortly after the Civil War, by the well-known Philadelphia architect James C. Sidney.

21   Muriel Grace Earhart Morrissey was born December 29, 1899, in Kansas City, Kansas, and died March 2, 1998, in Medford, Middlesex County, Massachusetts. Op. cit., 137.

22   Long missing, this dog was replaced with two, reclining, bronze dogs donated by cousin Virginia Tonsing of Mission, Kansas.

23   There were several clocks in the Martin-Tonsing house, but I suspect that the one most accessible to Amelia was the 1880s Seth Thomas clock on the mantle of the fireplace in the dining room. It was jet black adamantine or slate with three columns on each side of the gold frame of the dial. A brass lion's head was on

either end. The backplate could easily be removed and the pendulum and works removed for Amelia to examine.

25 Orpah Tonsing was born January 8, 1896, in Beloit, Kansas, and died February 6, 1973, in Leesburg, Florida. She married Parl L. Mellenbruch on January 28, 1918. Ibid., 122. The name, Orpah, is from the woman mentioned in Ruth 1:4 ff., who was the daughter-in-law of Naomi and sister of Ruth.

26 Ibid., 122.

27 "Amelia Earhart," Atchison Daily *Globe* (July 15, 1937).

28 "Bloomer, Amelia," *Encyclopedia Britannica* (Chicago: Encyclopedia Britannica, 1963).

29 Ida Challiss Martin entertained Helen M. Gouger, one of the most persistent advocates of woman's suffrage, and corresponded with her, according to her diary. Ida Challiss Martin, *Diary* (March 18, 19, 1887). It is also quite probable that she met Susan B. Anthony, Elizabeth Cady Stanton and Lucy Stone during their crusades in Kansas. "Ida Martin Writes Mrs. Gougar," and, "Ida Martin Persuades Governor Not to Veto Suffrage Bill," *Daily Globe*, Atchison, Kansas (March 22, 1887).

30 Amy Otis Earhart, letter to Ruth Martin Tonsing (April 8, 1942). I returned the letter to my grandmother that day; its present location is not known.

31 Ibid.

32 This was probably the "Seventh Coalition" of 1815

when England, Sweden, Russia, Prussia, Austria, the Netherlands and some German states allied their forces against France.

33   Amy Earhart, letter.

34   A writing slate was a thin plate of fine-grained, black stone encased in a wood frame 4x6 to 7x10 inches, that was used well into the twentieth century by schoolchildren to write their spelling or arithmetic lessons in chalk.

35   Muriel Earhart Morrissey, *Courage is the Price. The Biography of Amelia Earhart* (Wichita, Kansas: McCormick-Armstrong Publishing Division, 1963), 12.

36   Ibid., 12-13.

37   Amy Earhart, letter.

38   Maria Grace Harres (born August 2, 1797, Germantown, Philadelphia, Pennsylvania. She died September 17, 1896, in Atchison, Kansas. Martin and Chaky, 13.

39   Ibid.

40   Ibid.

41   Ibid. Deborah Ducoff-Barone wrote that Gebhard Harres had his business at 6 South Front St., Philadelphia, in 1825, and enlarged his manufacturing plant in 1830. He occupied a three-story rowhouse (which he owned) communicating with a three-story frame cabinetmaker's shop, which he rented from Christ Church in 1828 for $325 per year for six years. "Philadelphia Furniture Makers 1816-1830," *Antiques*, May 1,

1994. Beatsie Challiss Laws (communication, August 21, 2000), notes that Gebhard and Maria Grace Harres lived at 353 South 3rd St., on Society Hill in Philadelphia, at Chestnut Street and Catherine Street, until 1855. In 1857, the numbers on this street changed to the 180 block. In 1855, the couple moved to 10th and Catherine Street, on the east side of the street. In 2021, the Dante and Luigi Italian Restaurant at 762 Tenth St. occupies the three- or four-story building in which they lived.

42   Amy Earhart, letter, op. cit.

43   Ibid. The "Five Generation" picture shows Ida Challiss Martin standing behind her daughter, Ruth Martin Tonsing, who is holding Evan Walker Tonsing. Mary Ann Harres Challiss is on the left, and Maria Grace Harres on the right.

44   Passport application of Gebhard Harres (U.S. Passport Applications, 1895-1925).

45   Amy Earhart letter, op. cit.

46   Ibid.

47   William Sloane Kennedy, *Wonders and Curiosities of the Railway or Stories of the Locomotive in Every Land* (New York: S. C. Griggs and Company, 1884; New York: Hurst and Company, 1906), 120-1.

48   Ibid., 121-2.

49   The engraving appears in Kennedy. Ibid., 123.

50   "Tom Thumb (locomotive)," *Wikipedia* (accessed March 15, 2010).

51 "Early Railroad Transportation, *Philadelphia History*, http://74.125.155.132/ search?q=cache:7q4cHdxhONAJ:www.ushistory.org/ Philadelphia/+%22Philadelphia+history%22+%2B+ %22Early+Railroad+Transportation%22&cd=4&hl =en&ct=clnk&gl=us (accessed March 12, 2010).

52 Ibid.

53 Ibid.

54 William Sloane Kennedy, *Wonders and Curiosities of the Railway or Stories of the Locomotive in Every Land* (New York: S. C. Griggs and Company, 1884; New York: Hurst and Company, 1906), 53.

55 Ibid. The engraving is copyrighted 1883 by Hoopes and Townsend, Philadelphia.

56 Thus, the four cars of the train on November 24, 1832, would have held some eighty passengers.

57 "Baldwin Locomotive Works," *Wikipedia* (accessed March 8, 2010).

58 "Matthias W. Baldwin, *Wikipedia* (accessed March 8, 2010).

59 "Railroads America—The De Witt Clinton and Old Ironsides" (originally published 1927), http:// www.oldandsold.com/articles25/railroads-16.shtml (accessed March 8, 2010).

60 Kennedy, 52.

61 William H. Brown, *The History of the First Locomotives in America* (New York: D. Appleton & Co., 1871),

Chapter 33 (online).

62 Ibid.

63 Ibid.

64 "Railroads America" (1927).

65 Ibid.

66 Ibid.

67 Amy Earhart Letter, op. cit.

68 Ibid. When Gebhard and Maria Grace visited their daughters, Mary Ann Harres Challiss and Amelia Harres Otis in Atchison, he suddenly died May 23, 1863. His body was shipped back to Philadelphia where it was buried in Lot 44, Section X, of Laurel Hill Cemetery. Maria Grace sold their home and moved to Atchison to the Alfred and Amelia Otis house where she lived to the age of 99.

69 Chaky and Martin, op. cit., 133.

70 David Earhart died August 13, 1903, and his wife, Mary Wells Patton Earhart, May 19, 1893. Ibid.

71 H.J. Ott, *A History of the Evangelical Lutheran Synod of Kansas (General Synod), Together With a Sketch of the Augustana Synod Churches and a Brief Presentation of Other Lutheran Bodies Located in Kansas* (Topeka, Kansas: F. M. Steves & Sons, for the Kansas Synod, 1907).

72 David Earhart, *Journal 1845-1875*. I am indebted to Louise Foudray, caretaker of the Amelia Earhart

Birthplace Museum, Atchison, Kansas, for sending me a photocopy of this journal.

73 This is mentioned in the entries of June 14, 1845; October 26, 1846; December 28, 1846; February 24, 1847; October 7, 1847; February 15, 1848; and September 5, 1848, etc.

74 Copies of these books may be seen at the Kansas State Historical Society Archives in Topeka, Kansas.

75 Sarah Catherine Earhart was born August 21, 1849, and died October 30, 1851. Chaky and Martin, op. cit., 133-134.

76 Laid out in 1855 and incorporated in 1869, the town was named after a nearby waterfall in the Grasshopper River. After the grasshopper invasion in the 1870s, however, the people of Grasshopper Falls realized that the odd name of the town would not attract new settlers, so they changed the name to Valley Falls and the river to the Delaware River. However, the county remains Grasshopper Falls County.

77 Ott, *History*, 18.

78 The Rev. Pardee Butler, a Methodist pastor, gave accounts of his conflicts with the pro-slavery "ruffians" in the Kansas Territory in lengthy articles in the Atchison, Kansas, *Champion* (April 1881, ff.), edited by John A. Martin, husband of Ida Challiss Martin and a cousin of Amelia's mother. Pardee Butler, "Pardee Butler's History of Atchison," Daily *Champion*, Atchison Kansas (June 9, 1881).

79 Ott, *History*, 18-19.

80 Kansas House of Representatives Resolution No. 6005, *Journal* (January 31, 1997).

81 Ott, *History*, 18-19.

82 Ibid., 19.

83 Ibid., 20.

84 Ibid., 21. "Bilious fever" is a term for any fever that is accompanied by nausea and strong diarrhea.

85 Ott, *History of the Lutheran Synod of Kansas*, 29.

86 Ibid., 28-29.

87 The Rev. J. B. McAfee, in, Ott, ibid., 20-21.

88 Ibid., 18. Nestor, king of Pylos, participated in the Trojan War with the Achaeans, and, while too old to engage in combat, he was revered for his leadership, bravery, and speaking abilities.

89 Harriet Earhart was born in 1842 and died in 1927. She married Aaron Monroe in 1865. Chaky and Martin, 134.

90 Harriet Earhart Monroe is not even mentioned in Doris L. Rich's *Amelia Earhart. A Biography* (Washington and London: Smithsonian Institution Press, 1989); John Burke, *Winged Legend. The Story of Amelia Earhart* (New York: G. P.Putnam's Sons, 1970); Mary S. Lovell, *The Sound of Wings. The Life of Amelia Earhart* (New York: St. Martin's Press, 1898); Adele de Leeuw, *The Story of Amelia Earhart* (New York:

Grosset & Dunlap, 1955); Susan Ware, *Still Mission. Amelia Earhart and the Search for Modern Feminism* (New York: W. W. Norton & Company, 1993), etc.

91 Susan Butler, *East to the Dawn. The Life of Amelia Earhart* (Reading, Massachusetts: Addison-Wesley 1977), 5, 24.

92 Ibid., 24.

93 Mary Wells Patton was born September 28, 1821 or 1822, and died May 19, 1893, and David Earhart was born February 28, 1818, and died August 13, 1903. They married November 16, 1841. Chaky and Martin, 133.

94 In November, 1861, some 1,500 of Confederate Gen. Sterling Price's army arrived and camped opposite Atchison on the Missouri side of the river, announcing their intention to "sack and burn" the city. When an appeal for troops and guns from Fort Leavenworth brought them only a single cannon, the "boys" of Atchison assembled "Quaker" cannons, that is, stovepipes mounted on wheels that they had taken from wagons in town. Firing their only cannon, a lucky shot landed on the roof of a barn where the soldiers were sitting, causing a general rout, thus saving Kansas from invasion. "That Reminds Me," *Freedom's Champion* (January 6, 1886).

95 Eugene E. Monroe was born October 12, 1868, and died April 9, 1927, in Park City, Utah. Richard Tonsing and Margaret Bernard's Family Tree (online) (accessed May 20, 2017).

96   "Rev. David Earhart, Atchison," *The United States Biographical Dictionary, Kansas Volume* (Chicago and Kansas City: S. Lewis & Co., Publishers, 1879), 795. Monroe built a stone structure on the north side of the 300 block of Kansas in 1871, and then enlarged it in 1876 for her school. She also built a structure at the northwest corner of Third and Kansas as a dormitory for her students. After closing her school it became a hotel. *Atchison Kansas-Supplier to the West* (Mo-Kan Regional Council, n.d.), 12.

97   Frances E. Willard and Mary A. Livermore, *American Women. Fifteen Hundred Biographies with Over 1,400 Portraits. A Comprehensive Encyclopedia of the Lives and Achievements of American Women During the Nineteenth Century* (New York: Mast, Crowell & Kirkpatrick, 1893), 512.

98   The city of Atchison offered to the Board of Education of the General Synod of the Lutheran Church to give "$50,000 for buildings, twenty acres of land in Highland Park for a campus, five acres for professors' homes, a half interest in the sale of 500 acres of land, and a promise of 300 students." Ott, *History of the Evangelical Lutheran Synod of Kansas*, 231. The college moved to Fremont, Nebraska, in 1919, and later merged with Luther Junior College, Wahoo, Nebraska. It became a university in 2010.

99   Harriet Earhart Monroe, *Twice-Born Men in America, or, The Psychology of Conversion as Seen by a Christian Psychologist in Rescue Mission Work* (Philadelphia: The Lutheran Publication Society, 1914), *The Art and*

Science of Conversation and Treatises on Other Subjects Pertaining to Teaching (New York and Chicago: A. S. Barnes & Company, 1889).

100 "Monroe, Mrs. Harriet Earhart," Willard and Livermore, *American Women, Fifteen Hundred Biographies*, vol. 1, 513.

101 Ibid., vol. 1, 512. In Philadelphia she lived at 1706 Vine St., and subsequently in Washington, D.C., she lived at 204 A St., SE. Richard Tonsing's and Margaret Bernard's Family Trees (online)(accessed May 16, 2017).

102 The advertisement is at the Kansas State Historical Society Archives.

103 $1,000 is about $29,211 in 2021 dollars.

104 Handbill, Mrs. H. E. Monroe, "A Trip to Europe." The announcement is in the archives of the Kansas State Historical Society, Topeka, Kansas.

105 Harriet Earhart Monroe, *Past Thirty* (Philadelphia: No. 42 North Ninth Street, 1879).

106 Monroe, *The Heroine of the Mining Camp* (Philadelphia: Lutheran Publication Society, 1894), 7.

107 Monroe, *Historical Lutheranism* (Philadelphia, Pennsylvania: Lutheran Publication Society, 1895). She also discusses the predecessors of Luther, Wycliffe, Hus, Savonarola, Peter Waldo, Reuchlin, and Erasmus, and subsequent to Luther, John Calvin and Ulrich Zwingli.

108 Monroe, *History of the Life of Gustavus Adolphus II, The Hero-general of the Reformation* (Philadelphia: The Lutheran Publication Society, 1910).

109 Monroe, *Washington—Its Sights and Insights* (New York and London: Funk & Wagnall's, 1903).

110 Monroe, *Twice-Born Men.*

111 Monroe, *The Art and Science of Conversation and Treatises on Other Subjects Pertaining to Teaching* (New York and Chicago: A. S. Barnes & Company, 1889).

112 Ibid., 56-7.

113 Ibid., 45.

114 Ibid., 73-6.

115 "Rhoads Opera House Fire Historical Marker," "ExplorePAhistory.com" (accessed May 15, 2017).

116 Della Earhart Mayers was born in 1857, and was 51 at the time of her death. She is buried in the Boyertown, Pennsylvania, Fairview Cemetery along with other victims of the fire.

117 Harriet Earhart Monroe, *Twice-Born Men*, 7.

118 Ibid., 8.

119 Ibid.

120 $25 is worth about $715 in 2021.

121 Harriet Earhart Monroe, *Twice-Born Men*, 9.

122 Ibid., 9-10.

123 Ibid. A fire drum is a portable bin for burning wood.

124 Ibid., 10, 15 ff.

125 Ibid., 16-21. Chair seats were caned with fibers such as cane, rush, hickory bark, or even seagrass.

126 Ibid.

127 "Rev. David Earhart, Atchison," *The United States Biographical Dictionary* (Chicago and New York: American Biographical Publishing Co., 1883).

128 Ibid.

129 Nelson A. Mason, "Mother Monroe," *Lutheran Herald* (n.d.). The coal mining operator was named Baker. Harriet Earhart Monroe is buried in Mount Vernon Cemetery, Atchison, Kansas.

130 Chaky and Martin, 15.

131 Amy Earhart letter.

132 "A Good Trait of the Early Days," *Atchison Globe* (May 4, 1910).

133 Chaky and Martin, 16.

134 Biographical Sketch of Judge Alfred G. Otis, Atchison County, Kansas, *Genealogical and Biographical Record of North-Eastern Kansas,* Transcribed by Penny R. Harrell (1900) (KSGenWeb Digital Library, accessed October 12, 2020).

135 Email letter from Dr. Rebecca Chaky, June 4, 2013.

136 This $1,000 in 1861 would be worth about $29,888

in 2021.

137 "A Good Trait of the Early Days," op. cit.

138 *Abilene Chronicle*, in Daily *Champion* (June 28, 1878).

139 John A. Martin, "Judge Otis' Address," *Champion*, Atchison, Kansas (January 7, 1881).

140 Amy Earhart letter.

141 This $25 in 1856 would be worth about $774 in 2021.

142 "Atchison Steam Ferry," *Freedom's Champion* (April 3, 1858).

143 Ida Challiss Martin, "What the People Say: Mrs. John A. Martin," *Atchison Globe* (January 25, 1929).

144 George T. Challiss was born in the 1830s, and died in 1894. Chaky and Martin, 41-42.

145 Ida Challiss Martin, "What the People Say."

146 Ibid.

147 *Champion* (February 19, 1887).

148 *Globe* (March 19, 1887).

149 *Champion*, (February 17, 1887).

150 *Champion* (March 18, 1887).

151 *Champion* (March 19, 1887).

152 *Champion* (March 23, 1887). The efforts to register women were not entirely successful in the city. According to the *Globe*: "The women of Atchison did not come to the front in the matter of registering as

they did in other Kansas towns. In Leavenworth, 2,673 have registered; in Topeka, 1,200; in Lawrence, 1,157; in Fort Scott, 522; in Emporia, 524, and more than 337 (the number in Atchison) registered in many small towns." *Champion* (March 28, 1887).

153 *Champion* (March 19, 1887).

154 *Globe* (March 22, 1887).

155 Two photographs exist, one is the "Four Generations Pictures," and the other is the "Five Generation Picture" taken in 1894 in the Otis house showing Ida Challiss Martin standing, and Mary Ann Harres Challiss, Ruth Martin Tonsing holding baby Evan Walker Tonsing, and Maria Grace Harres, then 97 years old, seated. This photograph is on display at the Amelia Earhart Birthplace Museum in Atchison, Kansas.

156 Amelia "Amy" Otis was born February 1, 1867, in Philadelphia, and died October 29, 1962, in Medford, Massachusetts. On October 18, 1895, she married Edwin Stanton Earhart, who was born March 28, 1872, in Atchison, and died September 23, 1930, in Los Angeles, California. Chaky and Martin, 135.

157 "Amelia Earhart," *Globe*, Atchison, Kansas (July 15, 1937). Ruth Martin Tonsing, "Memory Book."

158 Muriel Earhart Morrissey, *Courage is the Price. The Biography of Amelia Earhart* (Wichita, Kansas: McCormick-Armstrong Publishing Division, 1963), 117.

159 Unnamed reporter, "Amelia Earhart," *Globe* (July 15, 1937). Ruth Martin Tonsing, "Memory Book."

160 Ibid.

161 Kitty (Martha Kathryn) Mellenbruch was born March 28, 1930, in Springfield, Ohio. She married Allen John MacKinnon, who was born July 11, 1932, in Boston, Massachusetts, and died May 31, 1991, in Palo Alto, California. Chaky and Martin, 129.

162 Ibid., 135. Ruth Martin Tonsing was born May 30, 1873, and died March 20, 1867, in Atchison Kansas. Ibid., 55. Kitty MacKinnon, interview March 28, 2012, Salem Oregon.

163 "Save Amelia's Bronzing Project," *Los Angeles Times* (July 25, 3002).

164 The Rev. Ernest "Ernie" Frederick Tonsing was born July 7, 1908, in Atchison, Kansas, and died July 13, 1995, in Topeka, Kansas. On June 1, 1936, he married Dorothy Peterson, born July 15, 1909, in Falun, Kansas, and she died May 15, 1983, in Topeka, Kansas. Chaky and Martin, 102.

165 Ruth Martin Tonsing, *Five Year Diary*, 1945. Tiffy Cappel, interview, February 12, 2012.

166 Tiffy Challiss Cappel, interview, February 12, 2012.

167 The substance of this conversation was later reaffirmed by my grandmother, Ruth Martin Tonsing.

168 Muriel Earhart Morrissey, *Amelia Earhart* (Santa Barbara, California: Bellerophon Books, 1982), 47.

169 The popular "Mark Twain's Scrap Book" was patented June 24, 1873, and published by Daniel Slote & Co.,

New York.

170 Several of these reside in the Kansas State Historical Society Archives, Topeka, Kansas.

171 *Sunday Item-Tribune*, New Orleans, Louisiana (July 4, 1937). Ruth Tonsing, "Memory Book."

172 "Scour South Pacific for Missing Fliers," *Atchison Daily Globe*, Atchison, Kansas (July 15, 1937). Tonsing, "Memory Book."

173 *Sunday Item-Tribune*, New Orleans, Louisiana (July 4, 1937). Ruth Tonsing, "Memory Book."

174 "End Search Tomorrow," *Atchison Daily Globe*, Atchison, Kansas (July 16, 1937). Ruth Tonsing, "Memory Book."

175 "Psychic Says Amelia Lives. Gene Dennis, Atchison "Wonder Girl" Predicts Aviatrix Will Be Rescued." *Atchison Daily Globe* (July 16, 1937). Ruth Tonsing, "Memory Book."

176 "Putnam Offers Reward For Trace Of Amelia's Plane," *Atchison Daily Globe*, Atchison, Kansas (July 24, 1937). Ruth Tonsing, "Memory Book." $2,000 would be worth about $36,500 in 2021.

177 Theodore Otis, "Atchison Relative Feels Amelia Perished At Sea," *Globe*, (July 14, 1937). Tonsing, "Memory Book."

178 *Atchison Globe*, Atchison, Kansas (March 23, 1944). Ruth Tonsing, "Memory Book."

179 "A Proclamation," *Globe* (July 31, 1937). Ruth Tonsing, "Memory Book."

180 The Atchison County Memorial Hall is a two-story, buff brick, Neo-Classical building in Atchison, constructed in 1922. It has been nominated for the National Register of Historic Places. "Jr." is Paul Martin Tonsing Jr., Ruth Martin Tonsing's son.

181 The Rev. Burris A. Jenkins was a nationally known lecturer, author and editor, and publisher of the *Kansas City Post*. He was born in Kansas City, ordained in 1891, and returned to the city about 1907 where he became pastor of Linwood Boulevard Christian Church, and then the Community Christian Church in Kansas City

182 "In Tribute To Amelia Earhart," *Globe*, Atchison, Kansas (July 31, 1937).

183 "Atchison Relative Feels Amelia Perished At Sea," *Globe* (July 14, 1937).

184 Marian "Mim" Overholser, interview August 4, 2014, University Village, Thousand Oaks, California.

185 Kitty MacKinnon, interview March 28, 2012, Salem Oregon.

186 Tiffy Challiss Cappel, interview, February 12, 2012.

187 Ibid.

188 Amelia Earhart Putnam, *20 hrs. 40 min.* (New York: Grosset & Dunlap, 1928). *The Fun of It. Random Records of My Own Flying and of Women in Aviation* (Brooklyn, New York: Braunworth & Co., 1932, repr., Chicago: Academy Chicago Publishers, 1977). *Last Flight*, Arranged by George Palmer Putnam, Foreword

by Walter J. Boyne (New York: Harcourt, Brace and Company, 1937).

189 Amelia Earhart initiated her own fashion label in 1933, designing clothes that were distinctively tailored, comfortable, and moderately priced. The line of Amelia Earhart luggage was produced by the Orenstein Trunk Company of Newark, New Jersey, beginning in 1933.

190 Amelia Earhart, *The Fun of It*, 158 ff.

191 Ibid., 143-144.

192 Chaky and Martin and Richard Tonsing's and Margaret Bernard's Family Trees (online)(accessed October 10, 2020).

Made in the USA
Las Vegas, NV
05 June 2021

24184655R00085